Mark Vincent

THE SIGIL SECRET

using magic symbols to
protect, heal and create

palaysia
WORDS TO LIVE BY

WWW.THESIGILSECRET.COM

© Copyright 2021 Mark Smith and Edith Hagenaar
Published by Palaysia Publishers, UK, www.palaysia.com
ISBN 978-1-9168946-0-0   First print run 2021

Disclaimer: The author of this book does not dispense medical advice or prescribe the use of any technique as a form of treatment for physical, emotional, or medical problems. Always consult your doctor or physician for physical, emotional or medical problems. The intent of the author is only to offer information of a general nature to help you in your quest for emotional and spiritual well-being. In the event you use any of the information in this book for yourself, which is your right, the author and the publisher assume no responsibility for your actions.

Image credit, and with gratitude to: All hand-drawn sigils © copyright Zoe Smith unless otherwise noted. All computer-drawn sigils © copyright Edith Hagenaar unless otherwise noted. © Copyright via iStockPhoto.com: Cover and page 1-3 Dmitr1ch; page 4 LongQuattro; page 6 Astrology: Adobest; page 7 Buddha: Gwengoat; page 7 Chakra: benjaminalbiach; page 9 Sunrise: Serg_Velusceac; page 15 Mammoth: dottedhippo; page 15 Man: BsWei; page 20 + 31 Fireofheart; page 120 + 122 ATZ; page 124 Adobest. Creative Commons License via Wikipedia: Page 5 Coins: Jpb1301; Page 7 Swastika: Zereshk; Page 7 Adinkra stamps: ArtProf. Public Domain via Wikipedia: Page 6 Alchemy table: Frater5; page 9 Philosopher's Stone: Frater5; page 121 Otfried Lieberknecht. Public Domain other sources: Page 5 Cloth: Rijksmuseum Amsterdam; page 5 Wand: The Metropolitan Museum of Art, New York. © Copyright other images: Page 7 Muluk: Symbolikon; page 44 Rose https://sigilathenaeum.tumblr.com; page 97 Saturn: NASA/JPL-Caltech/SSI; page 101 Sigilsuite; page 102 Sigilscribe.me; page 104 Protection: Marckus Antuan; page 104 Love: Christian Jimenez; page 118 Marcel Acrata; page 119 Joseph H. Peterson http://www.esotericarchives.com; page 122 Almandine: Edith Hagenaar; page 125 Reda Ben Adam. Image credit not found after extensive search: Page 8 via Clarck Drieshen; Page 9 Osman Spare sigils. Please contact the publisher if you own the copyrights to either of these.

Some names in the book have been changed for reasons of privacy.

Get <u>free</u> access to the download section:

- Protocol of Intent worksheet
- Essential Intents e-book
- Sigils Magic Number e-book
- Additional Sigil Methods e-book
- and more!

Go to www.palaysia.com/sigilextras

For Zoe

CONTENTS

1. SIGILS

Sigils, in their simplest form, are a graphic, visual representation of an intent, notion or concept. They are either a symbolic, or a pictorial representation.

Sigils exist in many places in every day life – even traffic signs and icons like toilet signs are sigils. All chemical elements have their own sigil, as well as planets and astrological signs. In these instances, sigils are used either as an abbreviation of an otherwise lengthy word or sentence, or as a clear sign that even small children, illiterates or foreigners can understand.

Company logo's are also a type of sigil. A simple example is the golden arches of the McDonald's logo – that welcoming logo, inviting you to come in. Think also of the Nike swoosh. I'm guessing that as soon as you thought of that swoosh, you also thought of the slogan "Just do it". In a sense you just experienced a minimalist version of sigils at work. Just seeing the swoosh made you think of the slogan. The sigil produced an effect – and that is exactly what the companies want.

In occult or magic areas, sigils are often used to represent and invoke other worldly entities like spirits, angels and demons. The four elements of fire, air, earth and water all have their own sigils (see image below).

water   earth   fire   air

A brief history

The notion of representing ideas within a symbol dates back to the dawn of mankind. The first written languages, like hieroglyphics, use symbols representing an idea or thing. Egyptian hieroglyphics could be said to be an early ancestor of the modern sigils. Some languages to this day employ symbols rather than words made up of individual building blocks (letters), the most well known of course being Chinese.

Other than for the use of registering texts, laws or financial data, symbols were used early on for divination purposes. Norse runes, as well as the Chinese I Ching, are an example of this. For centuries, dating back to matriarchal times, women have embroidered sigils onto clothing while chanting verbal sigils, to protect and safeguard its wearers, or onto samplers, with intentions for healing, fertility, protection and rich harvests.

Top: Magic wand with sigils for protection, Egypt, ca. 1981–1640 B.C. *Bottom*: 4 Falus Coin with Sigil of Solomon, Morocco, 1873 A.D. *Left*: Fragment of linnen clothing with sigils sewn on, Koptic, ca. 500-799 A.D.

Throughout the ages, versions of sigils have existed in art and architecture around the world. Sigils were used for protection of a building, for fertility,

or for health. Sometimes sigils were added to works of art or to buildings as a hidden message, especially during times of inquisition or when a certain truth could be seen as heresy. At other times, sigils were used openly, for example on coins.

Top: Table of chemical and philophical symbols, Basil Valentine's Last Will and Testament, 1670 A.D.
Right: symbols for celestial bodies and metals.

The Greeks started using sigils to represent astronomical objects and their corresponding elements as early as 800 B.C., and this led alchemists and scientists to create sigils to represent newly-discovered objects and elements. These sigils are used to this day in science, astrology, esoterics and magick.

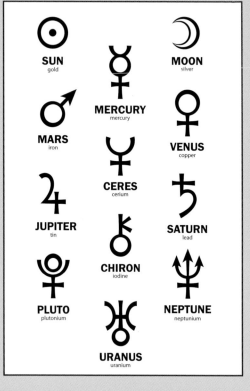

The idea of using symbols, or sigils, to protect, heal and create dates back to the matriarchy, and survived not just the test of time, but many witch hunts, inquisitions and other persecutions. Sigils have been and are used in cultures all over the world. The swastika is a sigil that is found as early as prehistoric times, and in cultures all across the globe. All major religions around the world have their own versions of sigils; Christianity has the cross, Islam the moon, and Judaism the star of David. We find the pentagram in Wicca and the Baphomet in LaVeyan Satanism. These are all versions of symbols that convey emotional meaning and are magical in nature. Medieval grimoires (magic books) contain many different examples of sigils.

Left: Buddha with Swastika sigil, Po Lin Monastery, Hong Kong. *Right*: Swastika's on a necklace, Iran, ca. 1200 B.C.

Top right: Adrinka sigils on stamps, Ghana. *Bottom right*: modern rendition of the Mayan Muluk sigil for rain, life force and prosperity. *Bottom left*: Pakua, the Yin-Yang sigil for balance surrounded by the eight i-ching oracle trigrams, China. *Top left*: Anahata, the heart chackra sigil, India.

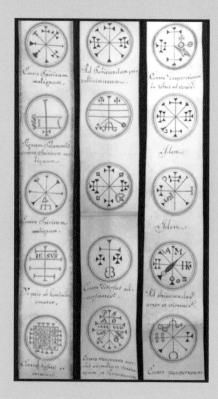

Magical sigils, copied onto an 17th-century English amulet roll, against evil spirits [1st column, 1st to 3rd rows], venomous snakes [2nd column, 5th row] and poverty [3rd column, 5th row] (England, 17th century): Add MS 25311. From https://blogs.bl.uk/digitisedmanuscripts/2019/07/magical-seals-in-an-english-book-of-hours.html by Clarck Drieshen.

The modern rise in using sigils is largely due to the English artist and occultist Austin Osman Spare (1886 – 1956), who developed a more modern kind of sigil, and the use of gnosis to empower these, based on his occult and esoteric studies. Chaos magic, a movement risen from the philosophy of Spare and developed in the 1960s out of a need to use magic without the religious connotations and based on results rather than elaborate, ornamental, dogmatic and ritualistic elements, has hugely popularised the use of sigils. The internet has further enabled people from all over the world to embrace sigils and their use is becoming increasingly widespread and common.

In this book, you will learn various methods for you to work with sigils to protect, heal and create, most of which stem from Chaos Magic – the system of magic that has no system. The basic tenet is that nothing is real and everything is permitted: whatever works to get you to the results you want, is what counts and is valid.

Top: Sigils drawn by Austin Osman Spare. *Bottom*: Sigil for the Philosopher's Stone or the Elixer of Life, for rejuvenation, enlightenment and bliss.

2. WHAT TO USE SIGILS FOR

The types of sigil in this book have a distinct purpose: they are a manifestation aid. These sigils are used to influence the world around you, to create change in accordance with your will and to allow your deepest desires to materialise by penetrating deep into your unconscious, bypassing your conscious doubting mechanisms. In this book you will learn how to convert your wishes, goals and desires into a symbolic representation.

Sigils are extremely versatile. You can use sigils to conjure everything from a small amount of money to career changes – pretty much any real world effect or goal you can think off. I have used sigils to help me join the right kind of musical group for me, for relationships, and for money. Sigils can be used both for physical as well as mental desires. Sigils for physical desires are designed to influence the world on a material level. They can be created to obtain things like:

- a house
- a partner
- protection and health
- fertility
- a job
- a status

Sigils for mental desires are designed to influence your sub-conscious and program your brain to act in a desired manner. They can be created to obtain things like:

- self esteem
- stop procrastinating
- creativity
- clarity
- calmness
- reaching a goal
- courage
- forgiveness

You can use sigils to help you nudge probability in your favour to acquire things that you want. Sigils allow you a mechanism for bypassing your doubts and ego-based objections, permitting your unconscious to seek out the things that you truly want. It also provides a way of bypassing any tendency to self sabotage. I find the biggest value is that they bypass my doubting mechanism, helping me release and let go of control.

You might want to work with sigils if you find yourself constantly blocking your own successes. You may want to try sigils if you have tried other systems and have had limited success. And you definitely want to apply sigils if things you want to manifest are important to you.

Sigils are used to help you magically acquire that which you desire.

Sigil for: Money flows to me in avalanches of abundance.

'In 2011 I lost my job and my house and had to move from the city. I decided to create my own personal sigil to find a good place that suited me, though I did not have enough money to pay any rent. After 2 or 3 weeks someone I didn't know contacted me to answer a message I posted, offering me a room. It was exactly what I had made the sigil for, even including the swimming pool I desired. And even better, a few days before that, a friend of mine from Germany had contacted me because he needed a copywriter urgently. I had the house and the job in less than twenty days with my sigil.' – Olibana, www.holistictimesblog.wordpress.com

'My mind used to wander everywhere, even when I was trying to concentrate on my work. Some thought would pop into my head, usually unrelated to what I was doing, and I would feel the urgent need to pursue that first. I did a sigil for concentration and after a few hours I already noticed a difference. Now, I am hyper-focussed when working.' –Aedith Empress

All is good

As discussed, a sigil enables you to spell cast your desire into being. In other words: sigils help you manifest your wishes. The nice thing about working with sigils is that you can't create anything unwanted. The very worst that can happen when you use it incorrectly, is that nothing will happen. When used correctly, what you want to happen, will happen.

All you are doing is activating certain parts of your brain to nudge the odds in your favour. There is nothing to be afraid of because the only thing changing is you. The use of sigils simply allows you to bypass that part of your brain that doubts that you can do the things that you already can do. There's just you, your beliefs and the result.

I know you'd probably like to get started on making sigils, and you *could* skip chapter three and fast forward to the sigil making part of this book – it's chaos magic after all: everything is allowed, there are no rules and no systems. However, successful spell casting is more than just executing specific tasks like devising and drawing a sigil. It is a process, wherein the actual sigil making is one of the final steps. The magical ritual consists of answering six questions, the making of the sigil, and the activation of the sigil. But even before we can start answering the six questions, you need to understand why and how sigils work, and what will keep your sigils from working, in order to get the best result from your sigil work.

3. WHY SIGILS WORK

The workings of the unconscious brain

I've been practising Sigil magic for a very long time. I started my journey many years ago as a teenager fascinated by Satanism. I still have a copy of the Satanic Bible and I'm quite a big fan of Anton LaVey, probably because I'm a bit of a contrarian: I'm not a fan of dogmatic systems. I have dabbled in what I hesitate to call "voodoo" and various forms of ceremonial magic.

Believing that results count more than anything else, and being a person who enjoys counter culture, I suppose it was inevitable that I eventually came across chaos magic and sigils.

Then I trained as a hypnotherapist and cognitive behavioural therapist. This allowed me to delve deeply into the nature of belief and the effect that conscious repetition has on our deep-seated beliefs. It allowed me, under a controlled environment, to learn methods of communicating with the unconscious, and to understand that the unconscious works in symbols and emotions. Most importantly, I became deeply familiar with the workings of the unconscious brain and how it is purely logical – but not even remotely rational. The more I began to understand these factors, the more I began to see the links with chaos magic. What is a therapeutic practice after all if not but manipulation of belief towards a result?

> *I've been a musician for many years and have used sigils in my career from time to time. My most obviously successful use of sigils was when I used them to join a band called Spearhead. At the time I was a little bit lost, musically speaking. I had been in bands for a long time, grown tired of it, and dropped out. I decided one day that I was going to audition for a band who advertised they were looking for a drummer. This band had a record deal and were reasonably well-known.*

I signed up for the audition but noticed that I wasn't actually learning the music. It occurred to me one day that this was because there was a little voice in my head telling me that I wasn't going to get the gig. At that point I cast my first sigil. The sigil was to help me enjoy the process and not worry about the result. "I enjoy the audition" was the Statement of Intent that I used.

I resolved to just do the audition, enjoy it, and make some new friends. From then on, I stopped procrastinating and learned the music for the audition – the sigil had managed to get around that little voice telling me I wouldn't succeed. I didn't get into the band, but that doesn't mean that the sigil failed: I did enjoy the audition, and that had been my Statement of Intent. After speaking to the guitarist from the band that I had just auditioned for, I asked him for recommendations for other bands. Whilst I didn't get the job with his band, the guitarist was very impressed with my playing and recommended me to a further 10 bands. I created a sigil for each band and got into every single one of them! Then I created a sigil with the Statement of Intent: "I join the band that is most suitable for me right now". One by one the bands fell away until I was left with Spearhead, the band that I ultimately joined and joyfully toured with for four years – I had joined the band that was most suitable for me.

While working with sigils over the years, I've spent a lot of time thinking about how to achieve a particular result. In this chapter you will learn why sigils work, but more importantly, the three things that will keep them from working:

1. <u>Lust of result</u>
   When the desire to get what you want is too strong.
2. <u>Being in the wrong state of mind</u>
   When you are anxious or stressed.
3. <u>Having the wrong desire</u>
   When there is a difference between what you think you want, and what you really want.

To understand why sigils work, we need to look at your two minds and how they work.

Two minds?

Imagine an immense mammoth, primal and ancient. This is the intuitive, unconscious mind – the limbic system. It is designed to safeguard your survival. The mammoth is the rapid thinker, reactive and primal. It is incredibly strong, incredibly powerful and incredibly stubborn. It's extremely resistant to change and panics easily in the face of overwhelming information. It lives in the now, cannot calculate odds and hates uncertainty. And it doesn't understand language.

Atop the mammoth is a rider. The rider is a medium-sized humanoid. It represents the rational, conscious brain – the frontal cortex. The rider can memorize, think, plan, talk and evaluate. It is the slow thinker, the analyst, the bit you are using to read this book. It is aware of linear time, hates uncertainty and uses logic.

The rider and the mammoth are two separate systems that only join quite late on in the womb, so it's very real to say that there are two of you.

Now looking at the image, which one do *you* think is in charge?

The rider might think he is in charge, but you will find in your day-to-day life various moments of your mammoth being in control. When you procrastinate over work – this is the mammoth sitting down and refusing to do what you tell it. When you get into an argument and you say something horrible that you don't really mean – that is the mammoth taking over and attacking for you. When you have a cigarette even though you had quit – that is the mammoth wanting to calm and sooth you. When you believe you are not capable of writing a book – that is the mammoth protecting you from wasting energy and disappointment. Even when you think the rider is in control, it just seems that way because the mammoth simply agrees with the rider. So make no mistake, the mammoth is in control. If the mammoth becomes frightened or doesn't want to do what the rider says for any reason, it will simply sit down and refuse to budge. If it feels threatened it will panic, become aggressive and potentially attack. Whenever the rider (conscious mind) and the mammoth (subconscious) are in conflict, the mammoth (subconscious) always wins.

But the rider can train and direct the mammoth.

The mammoth and the rider do not speak the same language but are able to communicate using symbols and feelings – the unconscious mind works in imagery and sensation, not language. If you make the mammoth feel safe, it will do whatever you want it to (as long as what you want doesn't threaten your immediate survival). If you panic and try and force the mammoth into doing things, it will become stubborn and belligerently sit down or even become aggressive and violent. Ignore the mammoth at your peril. If you ignore the mammoth's signals he is likely to run amok and cause havoc.

Sigils are a very good way of talking to, and directing the mammoth in a language it understands.

It is important to know that the rider – your conscious brain – needs a lot of energy to function. Sigils allow us to communicate with, and direct the mammoth in a more efficient way, because for the rider to try and direct the mammoth is hard work, and difficult.

So if we want to communicate directly and effectively with the mammoth, we can create sigils with our rider-selves to do just that: directing the mammoth and stopping it from self-sabotage.

But interestingly, we also need to bypass the rider. The rider, being the thinker, calculates the odds, analyses, and is rational. Where the mammoth uses feelings to self-sabotage, the rider uses ratio to self-sabotage. We need the rider and his realistic, calculating mind to not interfere. And again, sigils will do the trick, because in the process of creating sigils, we will strip them of any rational, analytical components that the rider could recognise and respond to.

So sigils work because they are images and therefore circumvent the rider. The mammoth recognizes the meaning of the sigil – the rider cannot – and enacts the instruction of the sigil.

> *Louise was suffering from panic attacks. In addition to this she was in a relationship that she was deeply unhappy with, with a partner who was very unpleasant towards her. She made a sigil firstly to ensure that her sigils would work, then she crafted two sigils, one for calm and the second for clarity.*
> *The panic attacks subsided within a week, and within a fortnight she had moved on from the partner who was wrong for her. By speaking directly to the mammoth she was able to calm and soothe the mammoth and get the clarity of thought she needed to move away from the relationship that was unsuitable for her.*

Beliefs and the RAS

In other words, sigils are used to influence the direction of your mind, and to program the Reticular Activating System (RAS). The RAS is a bundle of nerves in your brainstem, and its function is to filter information, so that only important things get through (otherwise the information overload would short circuit our brain). For everything we focus on (deliberately or not), it creates a filter that only allows through what meets our focus. So the RAS validates and strengthens our current beliefs, because it filters out everything that doesn't conform to our beliefs. If you think the world is a beautiful place, the RAS will filter only information that supports that – and subsequently, if you think the world is a terrible place, the RAS will only show you examples of that. When you deliberately program the RAS, it will then filter the incoming information specifically for what you have programmed it for.

Sigils are a great way to circumvent your current beliefs by programming the RAS to allow evidence of that which you have created your sigil for to pass through. Sigils, therefore, are great way of dismantling self-sabotaging beliefs either directly or indirectly:

- Directly dismantling a belief
  If you believe: "I will never be successful", creating a sigil for "I am successful" will directly dismantle the self-sabotaging belief.
- Indirectly dismantling a belief
  If you believe: "I will never be successful", creating a sigil for the next step up in your career, for example "I am senior project manager" will indirectly dismantle the self-sabotaging belief.

Sigils are also used to program the RAS to filter through information that will help you get what you want. If, for example, you want a new, specific house, the RAS will, once programmed, filter through all the information that will lead you to your desired home, like coincidentally meeting someone who is selling their house, or reading about a certain real estate agent.

So sigils will tell your RAS what to look for, and point your unconscious towards things that you want. Sigils are very good for situations where you feel like you want something, but don't think you deserve it, or don't know how to get it.

In the end, the entire process of the creation of a sigil deliberately joins emotions to ideas, to create real world effects. When you take put ideas and emotions together, you get reality – and sigils are very good for altering one or both of those factors in your brain.

Prohibiting factors

As discussed, there are three factors that hinder, if not prevent your sigils from working.

1. Lust of result

   1. Lust of result
      The first is known in chaos magic as *lust of result*. Lust of result is when you desire and crave the result so desperately that it becomes a threat itself. This results in the mammoth scared and unwilling to move, and is therefore the nemesis of the effective sigil creator.
      If you want your sigils to work, avoid lust of result as a priority. Managing lust of result is the single most effective thing you can do if you wish to be a good spell caster. The method of spell casting is much less relevant than your means of managing your lust of result. The first and most obvious way to tackle lust of result directly is to create sigils for the following:
      - *My sigils work*
      - *I forget my sigils*

      There is a free e-book explaining this in the download section, called "Essential Intents". The second way to clear any lust of result is found in the *Protocol of Intent*, which you will read about in chapter four.

2. Being in the wrong state of mind
   The second factor that renders your sigil ineffective is being in the wrong state of mind. When your are not in the right state, the mammoth sabotages your attempts. You may think the rider is in control when you

create the sigil, but in effect it is the mammoth who is creating the sigil – sometimes even forcing you to creating the sigil because it thinks it will make him feel better. This will lead you to create faulty sigils.

The first way to ensure you only make sigils when in the right state is to create a sigil for the following:

- *Before creating sigils I get into the right state of mind*

Please see the "Essential Intents" e-book.

3. Having the wrong desire

Earlier you read "Sigils are used to help you magically acquire that which you desire". The biggest hindrance preventing anyone trying to achieve a particular result, is being able to tell the difference between what you actually want and what you think you want, or believe you can have. These are three entirely separate things. In other words, it's telling the difference between what your rider wants, and what your mammoth wants (one could even argue that your soul might want a further thing).

In my example of trying finding a new band, it could have been my ego wanting to get into the well-known band-with-the-record-deal, but would that have truly made me happy? Finding out what it is I genuinely wanted – to enjoy playing and getting into a band that was most suitable for me – and basing my sigil on that, gave me the best possible outcome.

The first way to establish correct desires for your sigils, is to create a sigil for the following:

- *I find my true desire before I create a sigil*

Please see the "Essential Intents" e-book. The second way to ensure you are working with the correct desire is found in the *Protocol of in Intent*, which you will read about in chapter four.

Ensuring the power of your sigil

In the end, going through the motions of creating a sigil without having mitigated your lust of result, without being in the right state of mind, and with the wrong desire, is at best just a nice, creative way to spend your time. But this book is not about arts and crafts – this book is about performing magic by creating powerful sigils. It is to that end that this extensive section is dedicated. You'll learn how behaviour occurs and how lust of result, the state of mind and finding the right desire can be tackled.

The following model that I'm going to present is called the *Loops Model*. I spent many years attempting to come up with a single page explanation for how and why habits and beliefs form in the brain. The original reason I wanted to do this was to

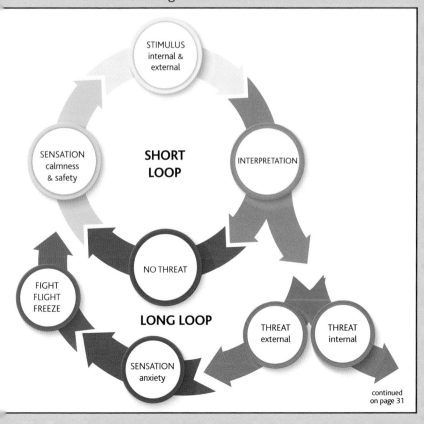

STIMULUS
internal &
external

SENSATION
calmness
& safety

**SHORT
LOOP**

INTERPRETATION

NO THREAT

FIGHT
FLIGHT
FREEZE

LONG LOOP

THREAT
external

THREAT
internal

SENSATION
anxiety

continued
on page 31

explain to people why an alcoholic simply cannot put down the drink and stop drinking – what it is that apparently compels the alcoholic to carry on doing something that would eventually kill him. This model is meant as way of thinking about thought, interpretation and belief.

Stimulus

The brain takes stimulus via the peripheral nervous system and through the spinal column. There are two main kinds of stimulus, internal and external. External stimulus is that which is happening to you right now – it's the sounds around you, the smells, the wind on your skin, everything you can see or experience through your five senses. External stimulus is in a sense what is "real" (I use that word advisedly in this context). It is what is happening right now outside of you.

Internal stimulus is your internalised version of what is happening. It is what you think is happening, or what you think might happen or has happened. Internal stimulus is more nebulous – it is a product of your emotional state and your imagination.

In my experience humans spend most of the time paying attention to internal stimulus. The ratio I give is 90% in favour of internal stimulus to 10% for external stimulus. That is to say that you spend most of the day walking around in your own head, not paying attention to what's happening to you. This is probably the single most important thing to understand about the human mind in this model: you spend most of your time inside your own head. However...

Your nervous system cannot tell the difference between internal and external stimulus and acts as though both are real.

Try the following experiment: recall a time recently when you had an argument with somebody or you felt bad about something, like a mistake at work. Notice that you start to experience the emotions that you would've experienced at the time. You'll

> *notice that you might feel a tightness in the chest, a feeling of nausea in the gut, a slight feeling of tension around your head as your body responds to the stimulus that exists purely in your mind.*

This is a very real phenomenon known as the ideomotor effect: if you think it, your body tries to do it. It is a key principle of hypnosis. There have even been tests done to demonstrate that muscle growth could be induced simply by imagining lifting weights. The thought of lifting the weights provides nerve stimulation in the muscle fibre as it reacts to the thought by contracting. Whilst this does not have the same affect as lifting itself, the very fact that it produces a response at all is extremely telling. There is a great deal of research done that has scientifically proven the ideomotor effect.

Quite literally your thoughts affect your body in a very physical way. This is no abstract phenomena and is very concrete and it happens all the time. It is how anaesthesia is induced in hypnosis. Suggesting that the hypnotic subject imagine that their hand is immersed up to the wrist in ice cold water will produce a mild analgesic effect in some subjects. The brain will then tell the nervous system to act accordingly to the perceived stimulus of cold water and will produce numbness in the hand.

Interpretation

The stimulus is then interpreted. Interpretation is always based on precedent. The brain takes the stimulus, analyses it and asks the question: "Did this happen before and what happened last time?" Precedent is the only way the brain has to tell it whether something is a thread and what it's appropriate reaction should be. This is why repetition is so important: repeated exposure solidifies the response.

Consequently, anything new is almost always perceived as a threat. This is one of the reasons babies cry at fireworks when they are first exposed. Repeated exposure teaches the baby that the noise is harmless and they learn that they are perfectly safe.

It's also exactly the same reason why you begin to worry when you're going to a party when you don't know anyone. Not knowing anyone at a party constitutes a threat as you have no idea how they will respond to you. Social isolation is also a huge threat to humans and our brains act accordingly.

Having looked through its memories and all the associations with this particular stimulus, the brain will then make a decision on whether the stimulus is a "threat" or "no threat".

No threat – short loop

If the particular stimulus has been experienced before, and the outcome was favourable, it is very likely that the stimulus will be categorised as "no threat". Then, parasympathetic nervous system is be activated.

The parasympathetic nervous system is part of the autonomic nervous system and controls automatic functions such as heart rate, hormone release, breathing et cetera. It is also known as the rest and digest part of your nervous system. It produces a feeling of safety and calm, so you can reproduce, eat and sleep. The release of serotonin, dopamine, painkillers and endorphins is associated with this part of your nervous system. Once the parasympathetic nervous system has been activated, you experience calmness and safety – a warm, possibly heavy feeling. Think of how you feel after you've had a hearty meal or when you're just about to have a nap.

Once the sensation has been processed the brain will return back to the stimulus part of the loop and carry on around.

This is called the "short loop", see page 21.

To go back to our mammoth and rider analogy, when you are in the short loop the rider is in control – you can make rational, focussed decisions, calculate odds, think creatively and solve problems.

The short loop is the ideal state for creating sigils.

Attempting to cast spells when not in this state is generally quite a bad idea. When you are in the short loop you can tell the difference between what is really happening, and what you *feel* is happening much more easily. You have energy to spare and expand on conscious rational analysis.

Threat – long loop

If the stimulus is categorised as a threat the brain will activate the sympathetic nervous system, and you enter the long loop (see image on page 21). This is also known as the fight or flight response and causes the release of adrenaline, noradrenaline and cortisol into the system. The sympathetic nervous system is the part of the autonomic nervous system that deals with escaping and destroying threats. The sensations produced by the activation of the sympathetic nervous system are acute, to say the least. Generally the sensations will occur from the base of the throat to the top of the pelvis, and can include tightness in the chest, a feeling of sickness, heat, sweating, shaking, accelerated heart rate, and so forth. All of these effects occur as the sympathetic nervous system prepares your body either to fight or to run away as fast as possible. Adrenaline and noradrenaline cause the pupils to dilate, the bronchi in the lungs expand and the heart rate speeds up. Cortisol breaks down tissue for energy at a rapid rate. It's quite literally like putting your foot down on the gas in the car or putting nitrous oxide into an engine. Everything becomes deeply focused in a single direction, everything points at the threat.

If you're not overwhelmed by the incoming stimulus your brain will then begin looking for a strategy, based on precedent: once again, precedent is the only way that you can have any chance of predicting what to do in a current situation. Your brain will search through its list of previous strategies and pick the one that will work the most efficiently and most rapidly based on past experiences related to the current situation. Broadly speaking the brain will pick either a fight or flight strategy: you will either try and destroy the threat or run away from it.

If the incoming data is too overwhelming however, you will shut down. Quite simply, in the absence of a suitable strategy the brain switches off, resulting in a blackout. It is the deer in the headlights effect, where you literally stand still, not knowing what to do.

The simpler the threat and the more immediate it is, the simpler the strategy. This is where the difference between internal and external threat becomes quite obvious. It's more likely that external threats are simple in as much as they tend to come out of nowhere, like being mugged or having to do a last minute presentation at work. The option of destroying the threat or running away from it (knocking the mugger out, or simply choosing not to turn up to do the presentation) are plausible actionable options.

When you're dealing with an internal stimulus however, those options are simply not there. Internal stimulus is much more difficult to deal with because in a certain way it is a phantom. Because internal stimulus is a product of your brain itself, it's very difficult to destroy and almost impossible to run away from. This results in you becoming caught in a resistance loop, I'll discuss that in more detail further on.

One of my favourite explanations for demonstrating how the loops work is the example of a smoker who is trying to quit. This is something that comes up quite frequently in my workshops, and I think graphically demonstrates all I've talked about before.

The first thing I should say is that stopping smoking is relatively easy to do. It's staying stopped that is hard.

To that end, as a therapist I very rarely work with people who are stopping smoking for the first time. I usually work with people who have relapsed at least once. This is because, believe it or not, the trick to stopping in the long term is learning how to relapse. In the first instance the person who wishes to stop smoking will create the internal stimulus, the idea that they want to stop smoking would be a good thing. This will register as a "no threat", as the initial idea seems like a good one, even though it's new.

The person resolves to stop smoking, throws the cigarettes away, and for about a week (maybe two if they're lucky) will continue on their merry way. At this point between 7-14 days into the process, the unconscious brain, the mammoth, realises that the conscious brain has made a decision that it intends is permanent. This idea of permanence is enough to elicit a "threat" interpretation.

In order to understand why this happens, we must examine why people smoke in the first place. Whilst I appreciate this is not a tutorial on therapy it is useful to understand the mechanisms that are happening here. Why do people smoke? Why would somebody do something that in the long-term will kill them? The answer is because in the short term smoking (and many other behaviours) has a meditative, calming affect. This is less to do with the inhalation of nicotine and more to do with the comforting sensation of something moving in and out of the mouth.

If one were to take a Freudian approach one could say that it goes back to breastfeeding and thumb-sucking in early life. However putting things into one's mouth has always been comforting. There is a reason why when people stop smoking they often put on weight. This is because this substitute the action of placing a cigarette in the mouth with the action of putting food in the mouth. It's less the act of smoking the more the act of having something touch the lips. The arm motion and the repetitious action are meditative and comforting. These are often factors that are overlooked when treating these problems. Any kind of repetitious motion is comforting because it is predictable. It creates an almost "mini belief". It's why babies will suck their thumbs. Why people will pace back and forth when they are stressed, victims will rock back and forth when they are traumatised and mothers will rock a baby to sleep in its cradle. It's why having hobbies like painting, playing a musical instrument or arts and crafts is so calming. They have a focused repetitious action that brings the brain into the present and calms it down. This is what cigarettes do for the smoker. They create a state of calm. They are a tool for *entering the short loop. The short loop means you are safe.*

Anything taking you out of the short loop is a threat.

So the mammoth realises that this is about to be taken away forever, detects that this is a very real threat and acts accordingly by activating the sympathetic nervous system and producing a huge stress response: insomnia, headaches, pins and needles in the hands and feet and large feeling of anxiety. This is often mistaken for withdrawal symptoms. Once the sensations have been produced in the body the unconscious will look for a way out strategy. It will look for the single fastest way possible in the shortest period of time to return to the calm state of the short loop. Accessing memory banks, looking for what worked last time, it quickly comes up with the answer: smoking.

Here is the paradox of stopping smoking. The harder you try, the harder it becomes. The more you lust after the result, the less likely you are to get it.

You're taking away something that made you feel better in the short term. Remember the mammoth is completely incapable of making long-term decisions, and will do things in the short term at the expense of the long term. The person eventually gives in, has a cigarette and resumes smoking. This temporarily produces a parasympathetic effect, temporarily calming the person down. Soon, however, they will then begin to experience thoughts of failure and guilt which in turn produce more threat responses, more sympathetic nervous system responses and more anxiety. The brain again looks for a solution to these and finds again that smoking was the most rapid way to stop the anxiety and related symptoms. Thus, the smoking increases. This is how the initial desire becomes a threat in itself. The more you lust after the result, the less likely you are to get it. The less you are able to get it, the more anxious you become.

This is the vicious cycle of trying to make something happen. The essence of lust of result.

> 'When I first started making You Tube videos, I so desperately wanted them to turn out perfect and create results for my business, that after a few videos I paralyzed and couldn't make any more. The lust of result was too high, and the thought of doing it wrong created such a thread that my mammoth just shut down.'
> —Aedith Empress

Worrying

We cannot reason our way out of this problem. The mammoth doesn't use words, only emotion. What do we do?

Let us briefly examine one more example of a loop in action.

> You're invited to a party by a good friend but you realise that you won't know anyone else at the party. For many people, the idea of going to the party and seeing their friend is quite pleasant, whereas the idea of not knowing anyone is probably quite unpleasant. The obvious social problems that come with not knowing people, the fear of being ignored, the fear of not being liked, will signal a threat. Once the threat has been registered the unconscious activates the sympathetic nervous system and the fight or flight response will produce a sensation in your body. Your brain will then look for a strategy. This is where it gets interesting.
> Let's say the party is two weeks away. Your unconscious is set up to run a fight or flight scenario, either to attack the perceived threat or to run away from it. The difficulty with this particular situation is that the threat itself is a phantom: it's just the idea of what might happen. If you remember that your nervous system cannot tell the difference between what it thinks will happen and what is actually happening, you can see how this could

be a huge problem. There is no solution that will give an immediate real world effect using the usual tools of fight or flight. There is nothing to attack or flee from.

One way that the mind deals with this is through the strategy of worrying. Worrying in the circumstances can be seen as a fight strategy as much as worrying attempts to pre-emptively solve the problem and therefore make it go away. The problem is that this sets up a self triggering loop. In order to think about a problem and solve it you have to think about the problem. If thinking about the problem causes you to be anxious you will send yourself into an anxiety loop simply by thinking about it.

This is why worrying only works in the very immediate term. In the very short term it gives a feeling of temporary safety and a sense of control as the mind gives the impression it's doing something about the problem.

However as I said before the act of thinking about the problem re-triggers all the anxieties. And so you get loop upon loop upon loop.

At some point frustration (lust of result) will kick in and create a another loop. Frustration (lust of result) that you cannot solve the problem which will bring up all kinds of other issues. This is a compounding problem and it's why worrying doesn't work: worrying just causes more worrying.

If it hasn't done so before, the brain will then consider the second option of simply not going to the party, employing an avoidance (flight) strategy. This can then set off further loops because if you really want to go (lust of result) but the strategy your brain is coming up with is to not go (causing further lust of result), you then enter what I have termed a "resistance loop".

Resistance loop
Resistance loops are sub-loops of the long loop whereby you have two contradicting statements that cause anxiety and exacerbate lust of result.

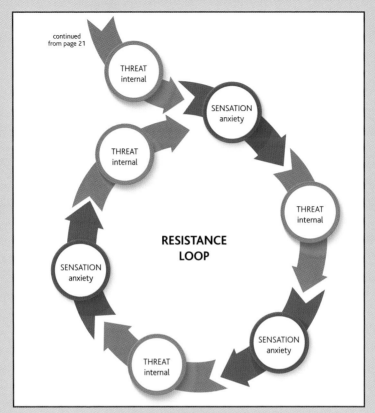

continued from page 21

THREAT
internal

SENSATION
anxiety

THREAT
internal

THREAT
internal

**RESISTANCE
LOOP**

SENSATION
anxiety

SENSATION
anxiety

THREAT
internal

Take the previous example: The mind uses a flight strategy to avoid going to the party, producing the paradoxical thought: "I want to go to the party but I don't want to go to the party."

These are two directly diametrically opposed statements. When you are in a resistance loop there is no logical answer. Solving one problem simply leaves you with the remaining problem unsolved. And in order to solve a resistance loop by thinking you have to think about the original problem (going to the party), as we discussed above, causes more problems. Resistance loops often occur with things that are emotionally valuable.

Resistance loops in this model are the essence of lust of result: the desire to have something but to not want it at the same time. If you run a resistance loop enough times, the initial desire eventually becomes a threat. Take the party example above: the idea of wanting to go to the party will trigger the thought that you don't want to go to the party (flight strategy) which will then cause anxiety that the brain will associate with the idea of going to the party. Eventually, the idea of going to the party itself is a threat.

'We had decided to sell our house because my husband had been unemployed for a long time and we didn't want to lose all our savings on paying the mortgage. I wanted to create a sigil for a smaller, cheaper house, but noticed I was in some sort of resistance loop: I didn't want to leave our house, but wanted to find a new house at the same time. At one point, even thinking about houses got my mammoth to panic and freeze.' –Jewel

Resistance loops and the rule of reversed effect

As you can see from the previous examples, habits and beliefs are developed through repetition through these thought/emotion loops. In order to fully understand how resistance loops work, we must first examine a psychological phenomenon known as the *rule of reversed effect*. The rule of reversed effect can be summed up as follows:

What you resist, persists.

Put simply, when you experience something that is generated by the unconscious, the harder you try to consciously stop it happening, the more likely it is to happen.

The simplest example of this is the statement: don't think of pink elephants. In trying not to think of pink elephants, an unconscious act, you immediately begin to think of pink elephants whether you want to or not.

This only become a problem when thinking of the pink elephant itself causes stress. The mechanism is exactly the same when you feel anxious about something but try and force yourself to not feel anxious about it. Or when you force yourself to do something that you don't really want to do.

This is often accompanied by sentences such as "I shouldn't do this", or "I must do this". The rule of reversed effect sets up and reinforces resistance loops.

> *Take for example the idea of wanting to stop smoking. After a certain amount of time when the brain recognises that the thought is real (permanent), it will react with anxiety. A resistance loop comes into play when the idea of not smoking is as great a threat as the idea of smoking. You then end up with a resistance loop somewhere along the lines of: "I must stop smoking but I can't stop smoking"*

The resistance loop is unsolvable by rational means, and doesn't respond to verbal endeavours. It is pure emotion, and an unsolvable conundrum. Once the resistance loop becomes apparent, both sides of the loop feed the other side in an ongoing anxiety vortex. In my experience resistance loops underlie all lust of result. They are very difficult to solve because they are driven by pure emotion and they are self reinforcing.

Another example would be: "I don't want to be anxious but I can't stop being anxious". The thought of not wanting to be anxious and being anxious will simply reinforce the level of anxiety by making the person feel like they have no ability to control their own emotions. This makes them feel more anxious and feeds the first loop because as they become more anxious the desire to not be anxious increases. This goes on and on and on and on. Until the loop itself is dictating behaviours.

The harder the person tries to stop being anxious, the more they run into their own belief that they can't stop, and the anxiety increases.

Why on earth would the brain do this? Remember that its only job is to help you survive. Safety and predictability are far more important than anything else and the unconscious, mammoth brain cannot think in the long or even the medium term, so will do things in the short term to keep you safe. It is better to be predictably anxious than attempting to introduce new stimulus by trying to solve the problem. This is why many people stay in these kind of loops for years and years, sometimes for their whole lives. Certainty is preferable to uncertainty, even certainty that can potentially kill you.

Breaking the loop

Effective sigil making can only take place when you're in the short loop. In order to get back in the short loop it is necessary to interrupt the anxiety process, to short-cut lust of result and to redirect the brain back to a calm relaxed state where, using the rider and mammoth analogy, the rider is directing the mammoth and not the other way round.

Now that we have a reasonable understanding of what lust of result is, how the brain forms beliefs and what resistance loops are, we can begin to formulate some kind of strategy. We understand that feelings are incredibly unreliable as they can be generated by internal stimulus which are not based on anything other than our own interpretation of what might be happening.

From what we looked at previously we now know that the brain interprets stimulus and produces sensations, in order to let you know whether you are under threat or not. So, these (interpretation and sensation) are the two main points at which we can break the loop.

I employ two simple techniques to break into these point and put myself back into the short loop, in order to achieve a suitable state for casting sigils.

1. Observation

This technique breaks the loop at the sensation stage. Do not be fooled by its simplicity: it's probably the single most effective thing you'll ever learn to do.

Once you have an understanding that your emotions are not "real" in any objective sense (they are mostly a product of internal stimulus, your own thoughts), it is useful to have a way to distance yourself from these emotions, to give yourself some mental space and objectivity. In order to do this we interrupt the loop just before the sensation part.

OBSERVATION EXERCISE

The first thing to do is notice when you are becoming anxious or resistant to an idea, thought or situation. Take some time to pay attention to the sensations in your body. The stress sensations will occur somewhere between the base of your neck and your pelvis. Notice the sensations. What are you experiencing? Is it tightness, heat, tension, pain? Where is the most prominent sensation? People often talk about feeling a tightness in the chest, noticing the heart racing or having a nauseous feeling in the stomach.

As soon as you have a moment to sit down, close your eyes and take your mind to the sensation.

Sit and observe the sensation.

Notice its shape. Are there any visuals? Is it static or moving? Does it have a temperature? What is it doing?

There is no need to name the sensation, just observe it as if you were observing an animal in the wild. Take a deep interest in it.

You will notice fairly soon that as you observe the sensation, it begins to change, often diminishing by quite a bit. This is simply because you are paying conscious attention to it.

The rule of reverse effect (what you resist, persists) works the other way, too: what you embrace, ceases.

The active observation diminishes the unconscious sensation and eventually makes it go away enough that you can think straight again. It's a simple way to take yourself out of the long loop and put yourself back in the short loop without even trying: the more passive you are on your observation, the more effective this exercise is. The harder you try to make the anxiety go away, the more likely it is to increase.

I suggest repeating this exercise daily. Become intimate with your own stress responses – these are the things that will sabotage your sigils. Become aware when you move into the long loop. You will find you go in and out of it all day. What are the warning signs? What are the alarms?

Once you have done this for a week or so, if you wish you can then begin to passively question it. One of my favourite questions is to ask:

What are you?

You can give the sensation a description or name at this point. You may label it anxiety, sorrow, fear or any number of things. By the simple act of labelling it, you are allowing yourself power over it.

This is a bit like a very controlled exorcism. Knowing the Demons name gives you power over it. The next time you get a particular sensation say in your chest, and you remember the previous time you had that sensation you were feeling sad, you will know immediately that you are probably feeling sad. You can then take the appropriate steps.

This sounds really obvious but many people honestly cannot tell exactly what they're feeling to that level of detail. In addition, by knowing what it is, it becomes much easier to let it go. Your mind will simply begin to recognise it as a repetitious behaviour and treat it accordingly. The mind realises it's "just a feeling" and over time lets it diminish.

If you wish to dig a little deeper, ask the following question:

What's underneath this sensation?

Ask these questions as if you are asking a third-party, and ask with no expectation of an answer. Very often when you receive an answer, it will not be verbal but occur as a sensation or a series of images. This is very individual and extremely subjective. Ask the question and wait. Sometimes you get an answer immediately, sometimes you get an answer within seven days, sometimes you get an answer within hours. The brain will answer you when it is ready.
Again by employing conscious enquiry you are activating the law of reverse effect to your benefit. The act of worrying or feeling anxious is unconscious. Lust of result is a by-product of these unconscious processes. Shining a light of conscious enquiry upon it, makes it process and diminish.

Another simple way of thinking about it, is that you are paying attention to the mammoth when it sits down. You're taking a moment to acknowledge that it is anxious, and like a pet or small child, sit with it until it has calmed down.
This is entirely in contrast with what most people do. Generally what happens is the person tries to force the frightened mammoth to move. This is entirely

counter-productive — the harder you try and force the mammoth, the more likely it is to stay put.

The third optional question is:

What are you resisting?

This is quite useful when you appear to have an anxious block but are not entirely sure of the source. Again, do not expect immediate or even verbal answers. Applying these questions will give you an insight into the root of the problem.

As a brief example, you may sit and notice that whenever you become anxious over a particular idea (smoking once again is a good example), you notice the tension in your solar plexus, in the centre of your chest. Paying attention to the sensation, you notice that it's dull, almost aching like it feels quite deep.

As you observe it, you notice that it has a certain amount of motion, and upon observing it for a certain amount of time it begins to dissipate upwards. It may even move into your throat and out through your eyes, causing you to cry. You name this sensation anxiety. Upon further enquiry, asking the question "what's underneath?" you begin to become aware that underneath anxiety is a certain amount of sadness and regret, a wish that you hadn't started smoking in the first place. Upon further enquiry you may find that there is guilt and a fear of failure. You will notice, as you ask these questions, every time you go back to the sensation it is slightly further diminished. As it becomes more and more familiar, it becomes much easier to deal with. You'll notice that you tend to go less into the long loop mode and stay extended periods in the short loop.

The conscious choice to observe is how you enter the short loop – the right state of mind, not just for powerful sigils, but for living a good life. In that state, you begin to find what you really want, which in turn will help you to create effective sigils.

> '*I started observing my emotions and asking the questions, and found both a sadness of having to leave the house with all its memories, and a fear of the unknown and uncertainty of moving somewhere new. The simple act of doing this, over the course of few days, got my anxiety down.*' *–Jewel*

2. Expressive writing
The second technique interrupts the loop at the stimulus stage and is called expressive writing – I often jokingly call this the apocalypse scenario.

EXERCISE
Firstly notice your thoughts, beliefs, objections and doubts about a given desire. Get two pieces of paper and a pen, set a timer for 10 minutes, and free write. When you're free writing I want you to focus on everything you think and feel about this particular desire, paying particular attention to the reasons you think you won't get it. Really go to town.
The only rule in this particular method is that you are not allowed to stop writing until the 10 minutes is up.
Really pour every doubt and fear, every anxiety you have about this particular desire, onto the paper. Think of all the worst things that could possibly happen if it goes wrong. Really dig into how you feel about this, what it means to you if it goes wrong or you don't get it.
Once you've done this, put the piece of paper away, and relax for five minutes – listen to some music, maybe make some drawings,

In the first stage we are paying attention to your sometimes hidden thoughts, giving them a voice. In the second stage we are applying our conscious mind and rationally solving them one by one. Using the rational mind to solve the problems gives emotional distance and increased objectivity.

This technique helps to avoid you entering into a resistance loop: you are specifically allowing time for the unconscious to express itself, and then specifically allowing time for the conscious mind to express itself. At no point are you trying to use one to stop the other.

Expressive writing is an extremely effective technique. One of the things you will find almost immediately is that the list of things that you thought you were afraid of is much shorter than you could've possibly imagined. You will be surprised at how easily you find solutions to most of these problems. Hint: if you get stuck on a problem, ask someone else for advice. This almost always helps, as its much easier to solve someone else's problem.

'I subsequently employed expressive writing and identified my hidden thoughts on moving and finding a new house. I then started to address these doubts and objections one by one. By applying these techniques, it became clear to me that I should create a sigil for "the most suitable home for us". After I had cre-

ated the sigil, my husband and I started to entertain the idea of renting one of our spare rooms out as a b&b, and though we had dismissed the idea before, we know became enthusiastic about it. And three days later, my husband got offered a new job. Long story short, we still live in our old home.' – Jewel

Summary

As you may have gathered, both these technique help you dismantle the three causes of weak and ineffective sigils. They get you out of the long loop and out of the resistance loop, so you get into the short loop – the right state of mind. They mitigate your lust, your craving for result. And they make it much easier to know what you actually because you aren't worrying about the consequences.

Even though you have to make your sigils when in the short loop, sigils do have the power to get you out of the long loop or the resistance loop – or better yet, to prevent you from getting there in the first place. So if you expect something in the near future to possible get you in either of the two longer loops, make a sigil to help prevent you getting there.

You now know why it is imperative that you get into the right state of mind before you start creating sigils – and how to get to that state of mind. That means you are ready for the next step: making your sigil.

4. MAKING YOUR SIGILS

Now that you have calmed the mammoth (see chapter three), you are ready for making your sigils. The making of a sigil can take as much as a week, or as little as 10 minutes – but the important thing is not to rush it, to take your time and to enjoy the process.

You might even want to prepare by meditating or getting yourself in a higher state of vibration beforehand. During the different stages of the sigil making, you can burn a candle and some incense, and play soothing and uplifting music. The idea is to make it into a wonderful, magical experience.

Making a sigil is and should be a very private activity, so if you are doing it with friends or in a group setting, be mindful of not looking at what others are doing and comparing your work with them. Besides, there is no such thing as an ugly sigil, other than in your mind, and a sigil does not need to be beautiful or aesthetically pleasing to be effective.

There are various methods to create a sigil, and we will start with the Spare method, named after its creator, Austin Osman Spare. After you have mastered this method, you can try out some of the other methods from chapter five.

The stages of making a sigil are:

1. Create a Statement of Intent
2. Create the formula
3. Chaosize the formula
4. Decorate the formula
5. Simplify the sigil
6. Seal the sigil
7. Fortify the sigil
8. Charge the sigil

In the next pages I will explain these stages in detail. Apart from the 5th and the 7th stage, all stages are mandatory for arriving at an effective and powerful sigil.

> *When you first start out, carve out some time to make at least three sigils in stead of just one. One of the main advantages of working with sigils is that they work like a trojan horse to bypass your conscious, rational, thinking mind. If you only make one sigil though, your mind will remember what the intention for this sigil was and when you see it, the trojan horse effect will be drastically diminished.*

Materials

When you first start out, I recommend just using a pen or pencil and some ordinary white paper.

Necessary:
- pen or pencil
- paper

Once you get the hang of it, you might want to introduce other materials, depending on your personal preferences, and you can make your sigils either more graphically aesthetic, stylish or decorative. You can go as far as making your sigil into a true work of art.

Optional:
- pair of compasses
- ruler
- drawing templates or draft rulers
- set square
- fountain pen
- calligraphy pen
- crayons, felt tip pens, coloured pencils, paint, etcetera
- coloured paper
- photograph
- canvas
- rock, wood, fabric, etcetera

Advanced options include:
- embroidery
- smiting (i.e. making them out of tin, silver, etcetera)
- carving in stone
- lithograph
- 3d printer

Use your imagination and develop your skills to create sigils of your own liking.

Incorporating your sigil into an existing element, like a painting, your front door, the mantelpiece, furniture, etcetera, is also an option. Some people carve sigils into elements in nature like trees or rocks – please only do this when legal and with the consent of the spirit of the tree or rock. Another wonderful way to make sigils is to trace them in sand, much like Japanese zen gardens.

A final option is creating the sigil on your computer, or even on your smart phone or tablet. You can either hand draw them directly into your computer by means of a drawing tablet, or use your keyboard to generate individual letters. The only thing you will need is a graphic software on your computer, like Photoshop, Illustrator, Sketch, CorelDraw, GIMP. Alternatively, you can use web based solutions like Canva or PixTeller. For your smart phone you can use apps like Infinite Design, Tayasui Sketches, Concepts, Adobe Photoshop Sketch, Autodesk Sketchbook, Infinite Painter or Procreate.

Sigil made with a 3d printer.

STAGE 1:
FORMULATE A STATEMENT OF INTENT

A *Statement of Intent* is a statement of something you want. In spell-casting we need to formulate a Statement of Intent in order to crystallize exactly what it is that we desire for the outcome. Good Statements of Intent ensure effective spell-casting.

Before we talk about good or bad, let's address your beliefs. If you let your beliefs interfere with your Statements of Intent, it may result in you not even making a sigil for what you want, but for something less. So when making a sigil and a Statement of Intent, really treat it as magic, as if a fairy godmother is swinging her magic wand and you get to wish for everything and anything you want. It might also be a good idea to make a Statement of Intent on your belief first, and only then (either directly afterwards, or a few days later) make a Statement of Intent on what it is you want.

> 'After having had migraines for most of life, and having tried everything to get rid of them, I noticed that, when I decided to make a sigil for them, I didn't believe at all it would work. So I made sigils for "I can eradicate migraine from my life" and "I know I can cure myself from migraines". Gradually, I felt my belief shifting, and I didn't create a sigil until I was convinced I could.' –Dennis

The statement needs to be precise enough that you can tell whether it's worked or not, whilst simultaneously not invoking lust of result or an anxiety response to the idea of the result.

A good Statement of Intent is what I call "vague specific". As an experiment in my workshops I often get my students to make a sigil to see a tall woman in pink heels. This Statement of Intent "I see a tall woman in pink heels" fits the bill pretty well. There are a reasonable amount of tall women around and relatively few of them wear pink heels. Pink heels are rare enough that they would be strikingly obvious when observed. This gives the brain enough information to know when the spell has worked but also reasonably wide scope of opportunity for the sigil to work.

It's very easy to formulate bad Statements of Intent. Statements of Intent, and thus sigils, work very literally. One of the worst Statements of Intent you can come up with is "I want a new job". If you don't specify at least some of the parameters of what the job is, you could lose your very nice office job and end up working in McDonald's. Even worse, you will just end up "wanting" a new job in perpetuity. Sigils work. Make sure you're being precise about you want them to do.

This kind of thing comes up several times in my workshops, probably the best example being one of my students who decided to get a new boyfriend. That was the only parameter that this person put in the sigil. He got a new boyfriend. However, the boyfriend left two weeks later.

He hadn't specified that he wanted a long-term relationship, and there was no detail as to the personality of the person. The sigil did what it was asked and planted itself on the unconscious, the unconscious then sought out a new boyfriend.

Sigils work. They do exactly what you ask them to, so formulate carefully. When we re-worked the sigil a second time in the workshop, we put in parameters and details around the idea of a long-term relationship. I'm happy to report this student is now in a long-term relationship.

The Protocol of Intent

Over the years, I have developed a method to formulate an effective Statement of Intent, and have taught this in my sigil magic courses and effective spell courses, that I've dubbed *The Protocol of Intent*. This protocol consists of six questions that are to be run in order on any desire you have, three times in a row.

You will find that by running these questions you will be able to come up with a clear, concise Statement of Intent that does not cause you any resistance whatsoever. These Statements of Intent will immediately put you in the short loop and allow for effective spell casting, particularly in sigil magic. You will find that when you follow the protocol as is given in this book, your sigil will gain enormous strength.

One you have completed the six questions, you will run them twice more. The reason for this is that the protocol does not produce solid answers on the first pass very often. It makes you think about what you're really after, brings up hidden anxieties as well as hidden wishes, and gives clarity and insight in a way that could turn everything upside down.

> When running the protocol brings up hidden anxieties or lust of result, use the two techniques outlined in the previous chapter to get back into the short loop.

It is likely that one or more of the answers to the six questions evoke resistance within you. A well known example of this is writers block: if you write a book then people will read it and might not like it. The brain decides is it much simpler, much safer and costs much less energy (which the brain feels is needed for your survival) to just not write the book than to take the risk of writing the book and having it not liked. Given a choice, the mind will always adopt the status quo – there is perceived safety in inaction.

> An excellent example occurred in one of my workshops when a student said that she wanted a room in which to start her business, but couldn't find one because "London was too expensive". The last sentence is very telling: the student believed that there

was no way that she could afford the room. Her belief was stopping her even looking. I asked the student what she could afford to pay and what she thought a reasonable amount was. I then asked where she had looked which unsurprisingly was only one place, which was too expensive. I then presented the student with two places where she could go and rent a room for the price that she found acceptable in the city (I have lots of contacts for places like this through working in the music industry for a long time and renting rooms to teach music).

The interesting thing at that point was the student experienced a huge wave of anxiety. She had got what she wanted, but part of her brain was resisting it. Following the protocol revealed that her original desire (a room for to start her business) was not really what she wanted. Getting a room to rent for the right price is a relatively easy thing to do and was literally staring her in the face. There was something else stopping her, and it came to light only by doing the Protocol of Intent. Having the room meant that she would actually have to try and make her business idea work, and she was naturally afraid of failure. Yet, her mind fixated on the financial issue instead of addressing the deeper fear of failure. Subsequently, she ended up making sigils to address her self-doubts and become confident about her business acumen.

Once you have uncovered your hidden motives, you can then examine and eliminate them by using the techniques in chapter three, or find a different strategy to meet their needs. The student could, for example, get coaching to overcome her fear.

Without further ado, let's get right to the questions. Get out a pen, your Protocol of Intent notepad or download the Protocol

 of Intent worksheet from the website, and start writing down your answers.

Download the Protocol of Intent worksheet here or scan the QR-code:
www.palaysia.com/sigilextras

Question one:

WHAT DO I WANT?

Write out your full desire into a Statement of Intent. At this point don't worry too much about it being a good statement — it is your first draft. If you fixate too much on getting it right the first time, you'll never do it. Just get it down on paper.

Much like affirmations, do phrase it in the present tense, make it active and use positive words. If you phrase a Statement of Intent in the negative your unconscious will reject the negative and hear a command. An example would be: "I don't smoke". The unconscious mind will reject the negative and will end up with a command "I smoke".

Unlike with affirmations, with sigils you can work with "unwanted words", like pain or anger. You should avoid it if possible, so always make an effort to find a positive Statement of Intent. If you do use an unwanted word, do not use it in combination with a negative like *can't* or *don't*, but rather in combination with the word *free* or verbs like *release* or *clear*. In the latter case, it can also be effective to add the word *need*. Some examples:

- I release my need for migraines
- I let go of my need for cigarettes
- My legs are pain free

Having said that, in these cases it is advisable to create multiple sigils, to work on the positives and wanteds. So to the above examples you could add:

- My head is clear and bright
- I am healthy, alive and kicking
- I breath clean air
- My legs are strong, healthy and feel great

It's perfectly fine to make statements that seem initially outlandish as the Protocol of Intent will reveal any problems and any inconsistencies, and will get to the heart of what you really want.

Most people will have multiple facets regarding their desire, and usually they will have more than one desire. A Statement of Intent that gets successful results however, should be short and limited to one desire, or one facet of a desire. Say for example that you want your children to get along better and respect each others stuff. It seems easy enough to have that sentence as a Statement of Intent, but actually they should be two separate ones: my children getting along with each other, and my children respecting each others stuff. You will want to run the Protocol of Intent on each one separately. That is the only way to guarantee you get the right answers for the right Statement of Intent.

Question two:

WHAT DIFFERENCE DOES IT MAKE TO ME IF I HAVE THIS?

Here is where you apply your creative imagination. How would your life be different if you had this desire? What would change? Think of everything, emotional, social, employment, financial; everything you can possibly think of, no matter how small, and both the positive as well as the negative consequences. Make sure to spend plenty of time on this – depending on the severity of your desire you might even need to sleep on this for a night, or three!

When one of my workshop attendees wanted to loose weight, she came up with loads of <u>positive consequences</u>. When she forced herself to find negative consequences, it was only after a few days that she realized that she would be 'unfaithful' to her sister, with whom she had this bond of eating together secretly, without her mother noticing. Unknowingly, her desire to have this special bond with her sister was more important to her than loosing weight. Because of this question, the hidden desire could surface to her conscious mind and she could look for different strategies to keep that special bond with her sister.

Do not be surprised if the answers to this question have an impact on your answer to question one. After answering this question, many people find that they change their mind about what they want.

Knowing what changes in your life when a desire is materialised, gives you a much deeper insight into whether the answer to the first question is really the correct one.

> *Here is a personal example to illustrate this. I was formulating a Statement of Intent for a sigil to improve my musical prospects and upon examination of the differences that would be made in my life, I realised there wouldn't be any – that I had everything I wanted already. I just thought I didn't. I have two music studios and I teach at a school, I have over 50 private students and the job that I love doing. I just felt that I didn't have enough.*
> *And that was the actual problem: I felt like I hadn't got enough. I started to work on a sigil to help me feel like "I have enough".*

Examining what difference the fulfilled desire will make, will help you to separate out what you *feel* is happening from what is *actually* happening.

You are keeping the mammoth from sitting down, or heading the unconscious off at the pass, by making yourself aware of what could happen.

Question three:

HOW AM I GOING TO OBTAIN IT?
Think of the different actions you could take to either obtain your desire directly, or make a start with moving toward the attainment of your desire.

What can you do right now immediately to obtain what you want? What can you do in the short term, in the next seven days? What can you do in the medium and long term? It's not unusual for people to get to this point and realise that actually what they want is staring them in the face and they just have to ask for it or go and get it. Very often in these situations, the simplest thing you can do is ask someone if they can help (see question four).

List all the ways in which you would be able to obtain your desired result. Take a bit of time for this question as well: your mind is not used to thinking in terms of possibilities, and it will need some processing time to come up with various options.

End your list with this statement: or any which way the Universe deems best.

> *Anne attended one of my workshops at Treadwell's books. She hated where she lived and desperately wanted to leave. She felt that she couldn't leave because she didn't have enough money to move house. She felt trapped and was constantly trying to get away from a difficult situation. We ran the Protocol of Intent. It turned out all that she needed to do in order to be able to move to where she wanted was to earn £40 extra a week. The protocol changed a huge problem into a very small, simple numerical problem. It changed from "how do I get out of this situation?" to "how do I earn £40 a week?"*
> *A sigil was made to allow her to earn the extra £40 a week and by the time the course finished a month later, she had moved.*

Question four:

WHO IS GOING TO HELP ME?

If you are no good at something or lack certain skills a, you should get someone else to do it for you. Most people are only really good at one or two things. And by good I mean really excellent. On a more mundane note, it is very useful to think "do I know anyone who would know how to get it for me?"

For example, if you are trying to start a business let's say as a business coach, do you have any contacts who move in those areas? Do you know anyone perhaps working in therapy or coaching circles?

It's not what you know, it's who you know. This works in spell casting as well as in business and many other areas of life. Knowing who can help you is extremely useful.

EXERCISE

Consider making sigils for people who will help get you ahead, to appear (see the "Essential Intents" e-book), or do the following exercise by creating an avatar for people you need to help you.
Sit down with a piece of paper and think of the ideal person to help you in this situation. List the following personal qualities:
  • What are they like?
  • Who do they know?
  • How would they help you?
Imagine in your mind exactly what this person will look like, every single detail:
  • How tall are they?
  • What colour is their hair?
  • What kind of clothing, shoes, jewellery do they wear?
  • What kind of job do they have?
  • Where do they live?
Then ask yourself, do I know anyone who knows anyone like this? How can I get hold of them?

Avatars are a kind of visual sigil in the mind. The brain begins looking for this person. The mind does not like unanswered questions, and the image of this person plus the desire to find them presents a question that needs answering. Many people often find that they know the people they need already and just haven't thought to ask them.

Now this *can* throw up anxieties and fears around the idea of asking people for help, being rejected, or being told you have a bad idea. These anxieties can be dealt with by making a sigil for it, and examining your beliefs by using the technique of expressive writing we discussed in chapter three.

Here is one helpful thing to remember: people like being asked for help. You are actually doing them a favour by asking for help because you elevate their social status by helping them be seen to be useful. Never doubt the power of this fact! Just imagine for a second someone asks you for help, for your expertise or opinion. Remember how good that feels – almost everybody feels like this. And now with the advent of social media and the internet it becomes even easier. Even extremely famous people are literally a click away from you. All you have to do is formulate a way to get to them.

James wanted a career change but was convinced he couldn't have one. We ran the Protocol of Intent upon the problem and realised that the area of work into which he wished to move, was one in which he already had a significant amount of contacts. Once this realisation occurred, James' underlying belief started to change and he began to believe that he could change careers. He posted a sigil onto LinkedIn and three days later was offered his dream job with a £10,000 increase on his current salary.

'Apart from people, I also look at what I call my heavenly help desk: people I knew that moved on into the spirit world. My grandfather, for example, was an author, and when I write a book I ask for his guidance. I will also ask spirits that I haven't known personally and are experts on the subject. When I was editing this book, for example, I solicited the aid and guidance of (the spirits of) Cornelius Agrippa (scholar and sigil expert, 1486-1535), John Dee (scholar and sigil expert, 1527-1608) and Austin Osman Spare (artist and the creator of the Spare method for sigils, 1886-1956).' –Aedith Empress

Question five:

WHEN AM I GOING TO DO IT?

Setting deadlines is good for the mind. However, I do want you to pay attention to your response to this question. If this question brings up feelings of anxiety and doubt, these need to be examined and dealt with, in the first place by making a sigil for them, and then using the techniques from chapter three. Picking apart your fears will start to reveal a pattern in your behaviour, so that you can more easily tell the difference between what you want and what you think you want. For some people deadlines are not an anxiety or resistance inducing idea, and if you're one of those people that's fine. I always set a deadline if for no other reason than seeing my response to the deadline.

Question six:

WHAT IS STOPPING ME?

The final question is the most telling of all. Having answered all the previous questions, you should have a reasonable idea of what it is you're after and how you're going to get it. Now you have to be honest with yourself: *What is stopping you?*

If you are lucky, the answer will be *nothing* and you will move towards what you desire with minimal fuss. This is common for simple desires like *Having a romantic evening with my partner*, but rare for more elaborate or complicated desires.

This question can stir up quite unpleasant feelings, and will bring out all the anxieties and fears not yet found in the previous questions. Understanding what is stopping you is a huge step in attaining what you want. In my experience people often get to this stage and then decide they're going to sigilise the thing stopping them first. Again, examining your thoughts by expressive writing and observing and questioning your feelings is very useful and tends to be extremely revealing.

Once you have run the protocol through for the first time, you should have a coherent Statement of Intent. It should be emotionally calm, relatively precise and time constrained. It is very common to run the protocol on a particular statement and have a statement completely change. Even if that's not the case, you should keep running the protocol until you are getting the same answers at least three times in a row — so yes, this is time consuming and can mean you run the protocol up to ten or even twenty times, but I cannot stress enough how important this is. The drawing and charging of the sigils are the least important part of this whole process — if you are not clear on what you want in the first place, the chances of you getting it are next to zero.

You are building the desire in your mind. Desire on its own is useless without method and conduit. You've got to know what you want and how you're going to get it and who is going to help you. In addition to that you're going to know what kind of things you're inclined to do to stop yourself getting on, and how you're going to overcome them.

This is the essence of a true magician. You lay out the rules of the game, change the ones you don't like and turn them to your advantage. This is how you will be relatively certain that what you're requesting is what you actually want. This is the difference between the short loop in the long loop. The rider (you) is in control, not the mammoth.

Do not think that this process is separate to the magical ritual — *it is the magical ritual*. The questions are the ritual, the sigils are the finale.

Example
My initial desire: to make a sigil for every desire I have.

ROUND ONE
1. What do I want? My first draft.
I make sigils for all my desires.

2. *What difference does it make to me if I have this?*
   My desires will be fulfilled. I will be more intentful of, and serious about getting my desires. I will experience magic in my life. Whenever I do make a sigil, I am always very pleased with the result, and looking at the sigils I've made makes me happy. Also, knowing the positive results the sigils I have done so far have given me, getting the results will make me happy.
3. *How am I going to obtain it?*
   Remembering to do it. Making time to do it. Giving priority to doing it. Realising it is important to do it.
4. *Who is going to help me?*
   It should be someone who is going to remind me and hold me accountable. Someone who doesn't think it is weird. One of my good friends. Or maybe a Facebook group, I wonder if there is a Facebook group for sigils.
5. *When am I going to do it?*
   It would be great to do one a day, but that may be too much in my already busy schedule. So if I did one once a week, it would become a great habit. I will pick Saturday morning.
6. *What is stopping me?*
   I'm not sure I've got the self-discipline. I might forget about it. I might not want to spend the time I will have to spend doing those 6x3 questions.

The self-discipline definitely calls for it's own sigil, but for the purpose of this example we're not going into that now.

ROUND TWO
1. *What do I want? My second draft.*
   I make a sigil every Saturday for a specific desire.
2. *What difference does it make to me if I have this?*
   As mentioned earlier, plus I would feel good about myself for being self-disciplined to do it every Saturday.
3. *How am I going to obtain it?*
   By calling it Sigil Saturday. By having a designated note pad for the Protocol of Intent.

4. *Who is going to help me?*
I'm going to post my sigil into a Facebook group every Saturday, so the group members will help me by holding me accountable and by cheering me on. I'm also going to ask a good friend to regularly check up on me, and I will post my sigils to her via WhatsApp.
5. *When am I going to do it?*
I'm starting next Saturday morning.
6. *What is stopping me?*
I might forget about it, unless of course I make this sigil.

ROUND THREE
1. *What do I want? My final draft.*
I make a sigil every Saturday.
2. *What difference does it make to me if I have this?*
As mentioned earlier.
3. *How am I going to obtain it?*
As mentioned earlier.
4. *Who is going to help me?*
As mentioned earlier.
5. *When am I going to do it?*
I'm starting next Saturday morning.
6. *What is stopping me?*
Nothing.

This is the sigil that came out of the Statement of Intent "I make a sigil every Saturday":

'My initial desire on which I ran the protocol, was about creating more time for my art. With five kids and a full time job, weeks go by without me having time to paint. When I ran the protocol I came to realize that what I needed above time was to overcome my procrastination – time seemed to be available, but I was using it as an excuse not to paint. So I started to run the protocol on procrastination. But then I uncovered that underneath that was a fear of rejection, and, my artwork being rejected, a fear of uselessness. So I ended up making sigils for feeling useful and needed, and for my art being loved and appreciated. I also did one on eagerness to paint, to offset any remaining procrastination. As a result, I find it much easier to tell my children and husband to do certain tasks and I now easily find time to paint.' – Tanya

Improving your Statement of Intent

Now that you have found your Statement of Intent by doing the Protocol of Intent, a further tweaking may be necessary to make your Statement of Intent – and thus your sigil – even more powerful. There are 5 ways to improve your Statement of Intent:

1. Remove White Noise and Parent Words

White Noise statements are statements that contain zero verifiable information and are not suitable for usage in Statements of Intent. Some examples of white noise Statements of Intent are:

- Do it better!
- The laundry must be done weekly
- I am
- God is Love
- It is better to think positive thoughts
- Calm down
- I'll try
- I love healthy food

White noise allows us to assert things that sound meaningful but actually mean very little at all. It is well worth paying attention to your own instances of white noise when constructing Statements of Intent, because these make sigils that have little or no effect.

Parent Words are the commanding words used by parents to children that are necessary in childhood, but get embedded in our unconscious and rear their ugly heads when we are adults. *Should*, *must*, *don't* are all examples of parent words. Often, parent words are used in Statements of Intent in combination with white noise. Take a look at these examples:
- I must do the laundry every week
- I should write a book
- I shouldn't drink so much
- I can't be lousy at that
- I must always think positive thoughts

When you have written your Statement of Intent, take time to examine it for white noise and parent words. So examples of rewritten Statements of Intent are:
- I do the laundry every Monday morning
- When in the shower, I think positive thoughts
- My book on ... is written
- I eat fresh produce with every meal

2. Examining your responses
Writing down your Statement of Intent will sometimes make thoughts leap into your minds, like:
- I can't do this
- This is never going to happen
- Not in my lifetime

In stead of ignoring those thoughts, question them by asking yourself:

HOW DO I KNOW?

It's a very useful question and uses the rule of reversed effect to a productive end. By consciously enquiring as to the evidence for the statement, you begin to unpick the limiting belief. Understanding that these statements itself are pure white noise gives you a place to start from.

How do I know? Most of the time you find you don't.

Is there a way you could know? Following up with this question often leads to productive outcomes. You are taking the unknown and making it known. You're taking something that is white noise and giving it clarity and definition.

3. Word Substitution

Word Substitution is an excellent technique to apply to both limiting beliefs and parent words. I'm going to give you one simple word to substitute all of these with. Whenever you hear yourself saying "should" or "must" or "can't" or any other variant of a parent word, I want you to substitute it with "could".

It seems like a minor alteration but it produces major framing changes in the mind. The statement "I can't do this" can be quite a threatening statement and it feels like it's true. Simply switching out "can't" for "could" is a gentle switch for the mind to begin to accept the possibility that maybe the first statement isn't entirely correct.

Additionally "I must do this" or "I should be doing this" are very self-punishing parental words that generally lead to huge amounts of anxiety. Simply substituting with "could" makes those statements more gentle, more open, more passive and more permissive. Going back to the analogy of the mammoth and the rider, using Parent Words is the equivalent of hitting the mammoth with a stick when it's frightened. Replacing the Parent Words with a more permissive word like "could" gives it pause for thought and a potential escape route. *Could* is a choice, *should* is a command. And the mammoth doesn't like being ordered around.

Take this example. You're on holiday and you think "I should be working at the moment" (this is particularly common amongst people who are self-employed): simply switch out the word "should" and you have the sentence "I could be working". It has an entirely different set of connotations and generally produces a much less anxious response. I could indeed be working, what else could I be doing? What would I like to be doing?

Try it for yourself: Say "I should be working" to yourself. Pay attention to the feel of the statement. Now say "I could be working". Notice if you are aware of the difference.

4. Further examination

Substituting "can't" for "could" also allows you to lead on to this question:

I COULD DO IT IF I DID WHAT?

Depending on the answers to this question, you may find you'll need to make further sigils. For example, supposing you were to make a sigil with the Statement of Intent: "I present with confidence, ease and joy." If writing down this statement gives you a thought like: "I will never be confident", replace with "could" to make "I could be confident". Now ask yourself: "I could be confident if I did what?" Answers could be: "If I loved myself", "If I went to a therapist or healer", "If I started small". Subsequently, make sigils for these.

5. E-Prime

To really delve deeply into analysis of your own language I like to apply e-prime to my statements. E-prime is a version of language that excludes all forms of the verb *to be*, including all conjugations, contractions and archaic forms.

E-priming can help make statements more accurate and re-move the illusion of objective certainty, and is achieved by sim-ply excluding the use of any variation of the verb *to be*.

For example, it is not possible to say "that is a chair" you would say something along the lines of "I perceive that as a chair". Whilst this seems incredibly cumbersome and in day-to-day parlance it definitely is not advisable, when it comes to magical practice, where precision is paramount, it yields a much greater power to your Statement of Intent – and with that, to your sigil.

When you remove all variations of the verb *to be*, you will find it quite difficult to make absolutist statements, and it ap-pears to become harder to be prejudiced in any way. You might even begin to notice the subjective nature of your own percep-tion, and this may help you in your quest to recognise your own psychological illusions. Ultimately, it helps you to better deter-mine the difference between what you really want and what your mind is telling you you want.

Take a look at these examples:

- I am confident
- My house is clean and tidy
- I am fit

After e-priming a more powerful Statement of Intent could look like this:

- Confidence
- Clean and tidy house
- Healthy, alive and kicking

The Protocol of Intent may seem like a lot of effort when you first start out, but the more often you've done it, the faster you will go through it. That's not to say you should rush through it, or do it on autopilot, but what you may dread now becomes easier because your mind gets used to the process.

> *It is all too tempting to skip the Protocol of Intent when you feel that you are in a hurry. But being in a hurry is a red flag for lust of result. Do the techniques in chapter three to diminish your lust of result, and take your time to run the Protocol of Intent. Note that you don't have time to not do the Protocol of Intent. Trust me.*

Summary

In order to prepare your Statement of Intent ready for sigilisation, you answer the six questions in order:

1. What do I want?
2. What difference does it make if I get it?
3. How am I going to get it?
4. Who is going to help me?
5. When am I going to do it?
6. What is stopping me?

As you are running the protocol analyse your statement for white noise and parent words. Additionally pay attention to any parts of the process that give rise to an anxious response in the body. Examine the thoughts that arise.

Repeat this process at least twice, and as often as you need until you have a Statement of Intent that is clear and accurate and that produces minimal resistance in your physical being.

DOWNLOAD YOUR COMPLIMENTARY PROTOCOL OF INTENT WORKSHEET AND LOTS OF OTHER EXTRAS FROM

WWW.PALAYSIA.COM/SIGILEXTRAS

STAGE 2:
CREATE THE FORMULA

Once you have completed the Protocol of Intent and feel that you have a suitable and, more importantly, powerful Statement of Intent, you can then proceed to the making of sigils.

In stage 2, you are going to create a formula from your Statement of Intent:

1. Write out your Statement of Intent
   I make a sigil every Saturday.
2. Remove the vowels, and rewrite in capitals
   MKSGLVRSTRDY
3. Remove duplicate letters
   MKSGLVRTDY

More examples:

- *Confidence* makes
  CFDN
- *House filled with love* makes
  HSFLDWTV
- *Money comes easily to me* makes
  MNYCSLT
- *My sigils work* makes
  MSGLWRK OR *MYSGLWRK*

You can apply the following rules for the letter Y:
Y is a consonant when it is used as a soft J, like in young
Y is a consonant when there already is a vowel in the syllable, like in key or Saturday
Y is a vowel when it is a separate syllable and produces a vowel sound, like in Bryan
Y is a vowel when it provides a vowel sound, like in system

or... use the Y whenever you feel it adds something.

STAGE 3:
CHAOSIZE THE FORMULA

Take a new sheet of paper and draw the letters you arrived at in stage 2 in random order, in random sizes, in random positions and with random orientation. The key here is randomness: you want to create chaos – an image your brain and conscious mind can no longer see as logical. What you are allowed, and even encouraged to do, is use your sense of aesthetics to create something that is pleasing for you to view. The letters do not need to be drawn individually: you can use the stem from an L to coincide with a T, for example, or make a K inside a D:

There is just one rule here: the letters need to touch each other, it has to be one element.

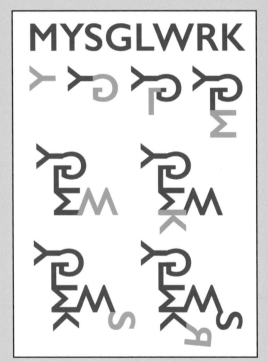

Left: Building up the image for "My sigils work" from left to right, by adding one (random) letter at a time (green), in random positions and random orientations.

Try out a few different ways to arrange the letters and see which one works best for you, or gives you the best feeling. As a variation, you can use lower-case letters in stead of capitals, but I have found capitals produce a more aesthetically pleasing image.

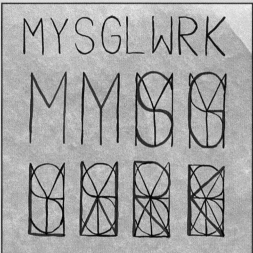

Top left: The final result of the image that was created on the previous page. *Middle left*: Building up a compact image for "My sigils work". *Top right*: The final result of the compact image. *Left*: alternative image for "My sigils work". As you can see, there are a great many ways of arranging the letters.

Another way you can vary, is to use multiple colours. Or, you can draw your sigil on a sheet of coloured paper or even a photograph. See stage seven for the use of specific colours.

Once you have your basic image, you can refine it as much as you like. Do not worry about how it looks and whether it's right or wrong, simply go on how it feels. Does it feel right?

For me personally, most of the time I take a very simplistic approach to making sigils and I usually use the first version that emerges. I've had students produce sigils in pencil on bits of paper in under 30 seconds, and I've also had students produce large oil paintings on canvas. It simply depends on your disposition, and how you feel it should look. This is very personal, and it's supposed to be. The science bit is over, this is an art.

Keep the Statement of Intent as far away from your image as possible, so by no means are you to write it underneath your image, or anywhere on the same paper. In order for your sigil to work, you are not to remember what its intent is.

When using the computer to create sigils, it is recommended to use straightforward, sans-serif fonts like Gill Sans, Futura, Avenir, Open Sans, Helvetica, Arial, Univers, Lucida Sans or Verdana, but it is entirely up to you and some people like using fancy, decorative fonts.

STAGE 4:
DECORATE THE FORMULA

As you can see, some of the lines are "loose ends" and float in the air. These lines need to be rounded off. There are two standard ways of rounding off a loose end: with a circle, or with a line.

Again, there is no wrong or right, there's just what feels good to you – the name of this stage is intentionally called 'decorate the formula'. Make your image even more pleasing and appealing to you, whichever way you like. Here are some examples:

Top left: Adding circles and lines. *Top right*: the final image. *Bottom*: variations.

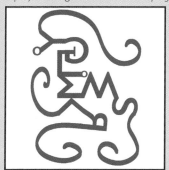
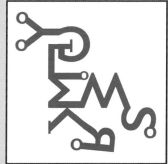

After you've worked with the standard circles and lines, you can add some personal variations if you want to make your sigil into a work of art.

STAGE 5 (OPTIONAL):
SIMPLIFY THE IMAGE

The fifth stage is optional, and I generally only use it when my formula contains too many letters, meaning that my image has become very large, very busy or complicated, or unappealing. If that is the case, there are two ways to simplify the image.

1. <u>Strip the formula</u>
   Go back to Stage 2 and remove articles, pronouns, adverbs, conjunctions and prepositions. If it is still too long, also remove adjectives. Continue with Stage 3.
2. <u>Striking components</u>
   Identify the components that seem to be most important and striking, and use only these in your new image.

becomes
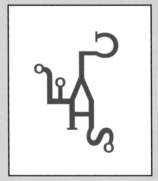

STAGE 6:
SEAL THE IMAGE

Once you feel that your image is ready, you may enclose it in a circle, triangle, square, star, rectangle, or any other shape of your choosing. Try out a few examples and see which shape works best with this specific image. You can even opt to double seal, i.e. to seal with two circles, two squares, two triangles, et-cetera, or first with a square then with a circle, and so on.

Once you get used to making sigils, you can take this a step further and use elemental symbols (see page 4) to enclose the image. To pick the right element, focus on your Statement of Intent and feel which element is most aligned with your intent. You can use this as a guideline:

- Material things, money — Earth
- Ideas, solutions, mind — Air
- Emotions, relationships — Water
- Health, energy, creativity — Fire

Or you can make even more elaborate seals, like is customary for the chakra sigils which are sealed with flower petals (see page 7). As a variation, if it feels better for you, you can leave the image unsealed.

You have now created your sigil, congratulations! We still have two more stages to go though, to activate your sigil and ensure it acquires its maximum power.

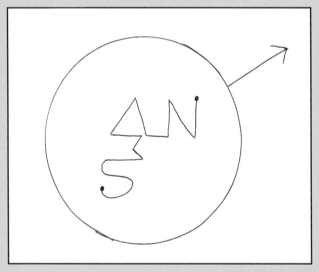

Sigil for 'I live my Soul's Mission', sealed with Mars' sigil for courage (see tabel of correspondencies on page 74), by Ædith Empress.

STAGE 7:
FORTIFY THE SIGIL

Stage seven, as was stage five, is optional, and if you are just starting out with sigils, you should skip this stage until you have mastered the basic steps.

The aim of this stage is to strengthen the sigil, and we do this by adding elements that correspond with the Statement of Intent, much like the advanced option in Stage 6. You can add physical elements like crystals, herbs, flowers and/or metals, as well as water, earth, air or fire (or better, something representing fire). You can add the corresponding colour or redraw the sigil in the corresponding colour, perform stage 8 on the corresponding day, or invoke the corresponding planetary energy.

Beware of not overdoing it, and don't go out of your way to add things: this should be a fun and light stage. Putting too much effort and severity in this will actually diminish the power of your sigil, rather than fortify it.

On the next page you will find a list with correspondences that you can use to determine how you can fortify your sigil.

'I made a sigil for my new business to prosper, and fortified my sigil with the correspondences for business, growth and prosperity: I charged the sigil on a Thursday, burned cedar incense, and wore my amethyst necklace.' –Barbara

'As an astrologer, I was a bit worried when Saturn entered my 7th House: it can either strengthen the commitment in a relationship or break up a relationship, but either way it puts your relationship under strain. I decided to make a sigil for my relationship and charge it on the day Saturn would enter my 7th House (which was a Sunday) but used Venus (love and relationship) correspondences, so I drew the Venus sigil into my sigil, had two roses and my rose quartz.' –Alexandra

Properties	Element	Colour	Planet	Day
Creativity; leadership; clarity; light; the self	Fire	Yellow, gold	Sun	Sunday
Emotions; intuition; tides; femininity; mother(-hood)	Water	Silver	Moon	Monday
Communication; commerce; travel; learning; teaching; siblings	Air	Blue	Mercury	Wednesday
Harmony; justice; love; beauty; partner(-ship)	Air	Green; pink	Venus	Friday
Energy; life force; lust; courage; assertion; conflict	Fire	Red	Mars	Tuesday
Harvest; rewards; income; success; values; seasons; environment	Earth	Orange	Ceres	Sunday
Truth; pushing boundaries; luck; greatness; law; education	Fire	Purple	Jupiter	Thursday
Mastery; time; perfection; abilities; restriction; father(-hood); obstacles	Earth	Grey	Saturn	Saturday
Health; rythm; purity; habits; daily work; organisation	Earth	White	Chiron	Monday
Vision; future; friends; internet; surprises; mental power; wishes	Air	Cyan (aqua)	Uranus	Wednesday
Art; inspiration; dreams; psychic powers; addiction	Water	Light blue	Neptune	Friday
Chaos and order; transformation; death; birth; sex; power; depth	Water	Black	Pluto	Tuesday

Sign	Metal	Tarot	Crystal	Herb
Leo	Gold	8, 19	Pyrite; sunstone	Marigold; saffron; dandelion; St. Johns wort
Cancer	Silver	2, 18	Selenite; moonstone	Willow; sweet birch; ylang
Gemini	Mercury	1, 6	Grafite; Opal; Hematite	Thyme; musk; rosemary
Libra	Copper	3, 11	Emerald; Peridote; Rose quartz	Rose; daffodil; myrtle; lavender
Aries	Iron	4, 16	Ruby; Almandine	Pepper; ginger; cloves; cardamom
Virgo	Indium; cerium	7, 9	Citrine; Aragonite	Cinnamon; chamomile; verbena; wheat
Sagittarius	Tin	10	Amethyst; Charoite; Chalcedony	Clover; cedar; patchouli; violet
Capricorn	Lead	14, 21	Saphire; Onyx; Dumortierite	Bay; basil; ashwagandha; mandrake
Virgo	Rhodium; chrome	5, 9	Smoky quartz; Azeztulite; Larimar	Camphor; iris; nettle
Aquarius	Zinc; uranium	0, 17	Labradorite; Chrysocolla; Turquoise	Forget-me-not; hemp; mushrooms; poorman's weatherglass
Pisces	Cobalt; pewter	12, 15	Aquamarine; Kyanite; Celestite	Frankincense; myrrh; acacia; sandalwood
Scorpio	Chrome; plutonium	13, 20	Cinnabar; Moldavite; Obsidian	Sage; cypress; lotus

The sigil we have been working on as an example, "My sigils work", is done in purple, but we want to harvest the result of our sigil work, so we are going to use the colour corresponding to harvesting and rewards: orange. We can see in the table that the corresponding element is earth, so we will seal our sigil with the earth sigil (see page 4):

STAGE 8:
CHARGE THE SIGIL

A sigil needs to be activated to powerfully manifest its intent, and we do that by charging the sigil with energy. There are five main categories of methods to charge your sigil. Each category has several different methods for charging a sigil – some of them are destructive, meaning that you won't have a physical copy of the sigil afterwards because it will be destroyed during the charging.

There is no right or wrong way to charge your sigil, just follow your intuition or be guided by the constraints of your sigil (evidently, you can't burn and destroy a sigil that has been carved into a rock).

You can also pick the type of charge by what corresponds with the intent of your sigil. If the intent of your sigil, for example, is to release something, a destructive charge fits perfectly. You can use the table of correspondences on the previous page to get some ideas.

Note: whenever you use fire or candles to charge your sigil, remain present until the fire has completely died or the candle has burned down, or blow out the candle when you are ready.

1. Fire and forget

With this category of methods, the point is not to look at the sigil again after charging, and basically forget about its existence straight away. If the method is destructive, you can take a photograph beforehand, but store it and don't look at it afterwards. If the method is not destructive, do not look at the sigil after charging, and place it in a box that you keep for this purpose specifically. You can look at the sigils after a few months, so it isn't absolutely necessary to destroy them. If you coincidentally happen to see your sigil again, for instance because it is still in the earth where you drew it, or the snow in which you drew it hasn't melted yet, that is absolutely no problem, but don't go searching for it.

Gaze at the sigil and focus on its intent for about ten to twenty seconds, before you charge it, unless otherwise stated, but don't think about the intent as you charge it.

By the way, to put it in the bin or trash can is not destroying it – the paper needs to be transformed by either fire, water, weathering or decay.

- Burn it
  Either make a fire, or use a candle to burn the sigil, and do this preferably outside, so the wind can dissipate the ashes and remaining shards of paper. If the sigil doesn't burn completely, just leave it like that and let the wind blow it away. I like to burn mine in an old tank shell that I have specifically for that purpose, simply because fire looks magical to me, and it feels right. Another option to burn it is by carving your sigil into a candle and burn it.
- Throw it in streaming water
  Throw your sigil in a river, sea or ocean, down a waterfall, or in any other stream in nature, and watch it drift away. If it doesn't drift away and gets stuck somewhere, leave it – don't try to push it back into the stream. After you've let it go, what happens with it is no longer up to you.
  If your sigil is on paper, you can optionally fold your sigil like a boat and set it afloat on the water.
  If you have no streaming water, you can also release your sigil into a lake or pond, if it is big enough.
  You can optionally draw your sigil with soluble ink and dissolve it in water in your garden or even indoors.

- **Throw it from a great height**
  Throw your sigil from the top of a canyon, a mountain ridge or from a tall building, and let the wind carry it away.
  Please use your common sense and do not throw rocks or other heavy materials from buildings or even down a mountain or canyon.
- **Bury it**
  Find a spot that either corresponds with your sigil's intent, or that you find beautiful.
- **Draw it in snow**
  A wonderful method for charging your sigil is to draw it into snow, using a stick or simply your finger.
  Alternatively, draw it with a warm finger on a frost bitten window.
- **Draw it in earth or sand**
  Another beautiful way to charge your sigil is to draw it in nature – it could be in the sand of a river bank or beach, in a forest, or even in your garden. In the case of sand, the tide will wash it away, but you don't have to wait around to see that happen. Just walk away after you have finished the drawing.
  Alternatively, you can draw it in chalk on the sidewalk when rain is forecast, and let the rain wash it away.
- **Draw it on yourself**
  Use felt tip pens to draw it on yourself, and let it wash away in the coming days while showering, bathing or swimming in nature or in a pool.
- **Draw it in condensation**
  While having a hot shower, draw it on the glass wall of your shower. Alternatively, draw it on the bathroom mirror after a hot shower.
- **Orgasm**
  Take the sigil and place it in front of you, masturbate or make love to someone, and, as you orgasm, stare at the sigil. During the state of orgasm you are unable to

think of anything and so the sigil is allowed to slip past your doubting mechanism into your unconscious mind. At this point, destroy the sigil.

- Eat it
  An interesting way of charging the sigil is literally bringing it into your system. Either make bread in the shape of the sigil, or etch the sigil into a pie. Bake it, consume it, digest it, and discard it.
- Leave it in a graveyard
  This a more Santería (voodoo) way of charging. Walk through the graveyard and let your intuition decide where and when to release it, or place it on a grave that appeals to you.
- Write it in the air
  A very old way of sigil charging was used by knights before battle: they would use their sword to carve their sigil in the air. You can emulate that by using a wand made of crystals or other natural materials (all wands need to be charged before their first use).
- Signal it on your body
  Another old way of sigil charging is used to this day by Roman Catholics as they draw a cross on their body with their fingers, before they undertake something important. So create the sigil by touching points on your face, chest and stomach with your fingers, lifting your fingers to go to the next point. Since the orientation of the sigil is irrelevant, you cannot make any mistakes, so don't worry about having to mirror the sigil. If your sigil is complex, think about simplifying it if you know you are going to charge it this way.

Please make sure that when you discard your sigil in nature, the materials used for your sigil are natural and biodegradable.

'I can never seem to bring myself to use a destructive method to charge my sigil, because looking at the sigils I've made just makes me feel good! When I wanted to increase the number of subscribers to my YouTube channel though, it felt good to ritually burn the sigil and let the wind diffuse the atoms with my intent all across the globe.' —Aedith Empress

'Depending on what I'm using it for, I sometimes keep the ashes and rub them on my intended "target".' —Christian Jimenez

We advise to only use positively stated Statements of Intent, but sometimes there is no work around and you have to use a 'negative' one like "remove migraines from my life". If you've made a sigil to get rid of something, like migraines, you must use a destructive charging method.

2. Meme and expose

The second category of charging sigils is to spread and display them. This is almost the opposite to the first category, as now you want to be exposed to the sigil, as well as expose others to it. The sigil will be charged when you no longer notice the presence of the sigil.

- Expose it
  If you've made your sigil into a work of art, expose it in a prominent place in your house, somewhere that you see it often. You can do this even if you've not made it into a work of art, but do make sure the sigil is large enough for you to see.
  Alternatively, add your sigil to a work of art that is already in your house.

- Wear it

  If you've made it into jewellery, wear it on your skin. Or, fold the paper with your sigil and stick it somewhere where it can touch your skin (like in a bra or sock). If that's not possible, the next best thing is to put it in a chest pocket.

  Another option is to sew it into your clothing.

- Meme it

  Make multiple copies of your sigil – you can use a printer with a copy function, or photograph and print, or reproduce them by hand – and place them in strategic places around your house, on your phone's background screen, as a screensaver or background on your computer, and in your car if you have one.

- Tattoo it

  A different way of wearing a sigil is to have it tattooed it on your body, and you can either choose to tattoo it somewhere that you can see it, or on your back. Do make sure, in the latter case, that others are able to see the tattoo, so don't put it in a hidden spot.

  It is of course entirely up to you to decide what to tattoo on your body, but we recommend only tattooing sigils that you are sure you want to be activated for the rest of your live, for example *safety and protection*, or *health*, or *I always thrive*. You may not realize now that some sigils, at some point, become undesirable.

- Spread it

  Another way to charge a sigil is to expose it to as many people as possible. You can draw it on postcards or letters and send to your friends and relatives. But in this digital age, the best way to do this is to photograph or scan your sigil (obviously, if you make the sigil on your computer it is already digital) and post it on your social media, use it as your profile picture, as a watermark on your You Tube videos, on your website or in your email signature.

If you post it on social media, consider every *like, share* or *comment* as an extra charge, but even without that your sigil will be charged as long as it gets seen.

You can also consider making the sigil barely visible, for example by setting the opacity of the image at 10%. This can be a good solution when the people you deal with are not into sigils or when using your email for work and business.

'I am a Taoist sorcerer who creates sigils for others. When I created two balance sigils for myself, I put all my belief into the sigils, and hung them in the front and back doors of my house. After a few days, I found that my life had found somewhat of a peaceful harmony. I never got along very well with my mother, but after the sigils were hung up, we started to become more agreeable to each other. Every time she called me, we had long conversations about our lives rather than arguing as usual. I found a balance between work and my friends whom I love dearly.' —Atish C., www.facebook.com/atish.ciriaco

Richard was given a parking ticket by the local council. In response to this ticket, he decided to sigilise to get it cancelled. His belief system holds the idea that other people can charge sigils for you. Instead of contesting the ticket, he simply sent back an envelope containing a "cancellation" sigil. The parking ticket was cancelled. Sometimes simple and direct works best.

3. Hybrid

This category offers some ways of charging your sigil, that need a second charging from either the first or the second category. Be careful of not overcharging your sigil by using too many different charging methods – use as many as feel right to you.

- **Manually charge**

  You can use Reiki or any other kind of manual practice that involves transfer of energy. You can opt to do it yourself, or have a healer or master charge it for you. Alternatively, if you are a religious person, you can charge your sigil by placing it by a statue or painting of the Buddha, Jesus Christ, or any God, saint or angel, or other element that is sacred to your religion.

- **Sunlight**

  Expose your sigil to a full day of sunlight and let the rays of the sun charge your sigil.

- **Moonlight**

  Expose your sigil to moonlight, and pick a phase of the moon that corresponds to the intent of the sigil: new moon for inner healing and new beginnings, first quarter for action and decisions, full moons for clarity, culmination and achievements, last quarter for release, freedom and happiness.

- **Crystals**

  Place crystals on and around your sigil.

- **Incense**

  Fan your sigil through burning incense.

- **Blood**

  Add your blood to the sigil. This works especially well when you have carved the sigil in wood or rock.

- **Pain and emotion**

  You can also charge your sigil by staring at it as you experience severe pain or deep emotions. Beware that you don't transpose the pain or emotion onto the sigil – this method is similar to the orgasm method and is meant to deeply embed the sigil into your subconscious, the pain and emotion are used to occupy your conscious mind.

- **Music**

  Bring the sigil to a concert and take it out when the orchestra or band plays your favourite part or song, a very emotionally charged part or song, or a part or song that matches the intent of the sigil.

Alternatively, sing to, chant, or play music for the sigil – the type of instrument is not important as long as it produces vibrations, so it doesn't have to be sound audible to the human ear.

- Dancing

  Place the sigil on the floor, and dance around it, with or without music.

- Incantation

  Create an incantation by taking the consonants you got in stage 2, mixing them up and adding one or more random vowels to get a pronounceable magical word.

  - *Confidence* makes *CFDN*
    makes *FENDAC*
  - *Long term relationship* makes *LNGTRMSHP*
    makes *PLOMHETGRANS*

  Now, take the magic number (see the "Magic Number" e-book in our download section), for this example we are using the number six. Recite the incantation six times, or a multiple of six, in order to charge the sigil.

4. Digital sigils

If you have used your computer or smart phone to make your sigil, you can either print it and use any of the above methods, or charge it with any of the following methods.

- Candle

  Leave it open on your screen and burn a small candle in front of it.

- Music and lights

  Play music on your computer while the document with the sigil is open, and put the luminosity and brightness of your screen to maximum.

- **Animated GIF**
  If you have a batch of sigils (see below), create an animated GIF, having the sigils alternate in rapid succession, while you stare at the sigils.
  You can also post this animation to your social media and on your website.

5. Batching

This is not so much a category, as a different way of approaching the sigil making and charging. We have discussed earlier that in some cases it is advisable to create multiple sigils, so as to address all the elements of a specific desire. This is called a batch or shoal of sigils.

Start making your first one, two or three sigils on day one, and subsequently make a sigil every day or every week (on the same day) until you feel you have covered all aspects related to your initial desire. Then, charge them in one go by using any of the methods from the previous categories. Or, alternatively, display one sigil in a large picture frame in your living room, for example, and use another method for the rest.

Here is an example of a batch of similar intents:
- Ease in public speaking
- I enjoy public speaking
- Confidence in public speaking
- I feel confident in front of group
- I am safe in front of a group

Make a batch of similar intents only to cover all aspects of a desire, not out of a need to be sure you've got the right one in there.

You can use this method as well if, after running the Protocol of Intent, you ended up with multiple Statements of Intent.

Another way to use this method is making a batch of unrelated sigils, because you know in the near future you will be travelling to a magical place that feels perfect to charge your sigils.

> 'From about two weeks before I left for my trip to India, I made a sigil every single day on different intents that were dear to my heart, and charged them by releasing them into the holy Ganges river.' – Jewel

Ritualize

When you have decided on a method for charging your sigil, you can extend it by adding a ritual, for example doing a meditation beforehand, dress in a certain way, bathe beforehand, call on your ancestors, invoke the angels, and so on. Or, for example if you raise energy into a circle, placing your sigils into the circle before you raise the energy and then using the energy of the ritual to charge them will work perfectly well.

You can also end the charging with a ritual like chanting, having a bath or shower, speaking words like "So be it" or "It is done", giving thanks to your spirit guides, and so on.

Adding your own ritual is not mandatory – some people prefer it short and quick, others like a more ceremonial moment, so do what feels good and natural to you.

Your own method

Use different charging methods for the first five to ten sigils you make. As you gain a good understanding of how to charge a sigil, you could even devise your own method if you want to.

Essential sigils

In the extras section with this book is a free e-book with essential intents. These are the best intents for you to start and practice with. The e-book also contain some intents that could be useful for the rest of your life. They do, however, require you to run the Protocol of Intent on them, to personalise and connect your own energy to the sigil.

Summary

Stage 1:   Protocol of Intent, three times six questions:
1. What do I want?
2. What difference does it make if I get it?
3. How am I going to get it?
4. Who is going to help me?
5. When am I going to do it?
6. What is stopping me?

Stage 2:   Create the formula
Stage 3:   Chaosize the formula
Stage 4:   Decorate the formula
Stage 5:   Simplify the image (optional)
Stage 6:   Seal the image
Stage 7:   Fortify the sigil (optional)
Stage 8:   Charge the sigil

Now that you have made your first sigils using the basic Spare method, we will dive into alternative ways of creating your sigil.

5. ALTERNATIVE METHODS

There are several alternatives to the basic sigil you learned in the previous chapter. In this chapter we will discuss the most important ones.

Gematria Sigil

Gematria is a type of numerology, which converts words into numbers and numbers into words with the aim of discovering hidden connections between different concepts. The assumptions is that an equal numerical value is meaningful and that two or more words (and thus, that which they stand for) with the same numerical value carry equal properties.

In order to make a gematria sigil, you need a cipher to code the formula you created in stage 2, into numbers. There are multiple cipher tables you can use for this conversion process, each of which yielding a different outcome. Choose the one that feels best suited to your Statement of Intent. With the digits you generate, you go back to stage 3 (page 66) and continue through the stages.

Pythagorean Table

1	2	3	4	5	6	7	8	9
A	B	C	D	E	F	G	H	I
J	K	L	M	N	O	P	Q	R
S	T	U	V	W	X	Y	Z	

Agrippean Table

A	B	C	D	E	F	G	H	I
1	2	3	4	5	6	7	8	9
K	L	M	N	O	P	Q	R	S
10	20	30	40	50	60	70	80	90
T	U	X	Y	Z	J	V		W
100	200	300	400	500	600	700		900

Classical Table

A	B	C	D	E	F	G	H	I
1	2	3	4	5	6	7	8	9
J	K	L	M	N	O	P	Q	R
10	11	12	13	14	15	16	17	18
S	T	U	V	W	X	Y	Z	
19	20	21	22	23	24	25	26	

English Table

A	B	C	D	E	F	G	H	I
6	12	18	24	30	36	42	48	54
J	K	L	M	N	O	P	Q	R
60	66	72	78	84	90	96	102	108
S	T	U	V	W	X	Y	Z	
114	120	126	132	138	144	150	156	

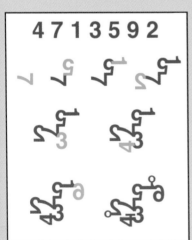

For our example Statement of Intent "My sigils work" we are going to use the Pythagorean table. So coming from stage 2 (page 65) we code MYSGLWRK into 4 7 1 7 3 5 9 2. Eliminate the duplicates and you get 4 7 1 3 5 9 2. We go back to stage 3 and carry on from there, but with the digits.

Left: Building up the image for "My sigils work" from left to right, by adding one (random) digit at a time (green), in random positions and orientations.

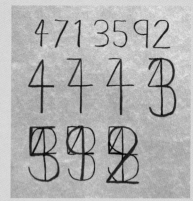

Top left: The final sigil, coloured and sealed. *Top right*: Building up a compact image for "My sigils work" from left to right, by adding one digit at a time (red).

You will probably have an immediate response as to whether you prefer the gematria sigil to the letter sigil, or not. I suggest experimenting with both for a while to see which you prefer.

There are also apps for your smart phone that will help you code your formula to a number, as well as a web-based service, at www.gematrix.org.

Hybrid sigils

Make a letter sigil and a gematria sigil. Then combine parts of both sigils to create a new, hybrid sigil.

letter sigil   +   number sigil   =   hybrid sigil

Kamea Sigils

A visually very different kind of sigil is created by using the Kamea method. A kamea is a square filled with unique numbers, of which the sums in each row, each column, and both main diagonals are the same. Because of their unique mathematic properties, kameas are also referred to as magic squares, even in science. An example:

	2	7	6	→ 15
	9	5	1	→ 15
	4	3	8	→ 15
15 ↙	↓ 15	↓ 15	↓ 15	↘ 15

The first seven kameas have been assigned to the seven classical celestial bodies, and thus convey their energies, properties and correspondences into your sigil. You can use the table of correspondences on page 74 to find out which kamea to use.

Even though the Sun and Moon are no planets, the term "planetary sigils" is often used in stead of kamea sigils. These are the seven celestial kameas:

Kamea of the Sun

6	32	3	34	35	1
7	11	27	28	8	30
19	14	16	15	23	24
18	20	22	21	17	13
25	29	10	9	26	12
36	5	33	4	2	31

Applicable gematria tables: Pythagorean or Classical

Kamea of the Moon

37	78	29	70	21	62	13	54	5
6	38	79	30	71	22	63	14	46
47	7	39	80	31	72	23	55	15
16	48	8	40	81	32	64	24	56
57	17	49	9	41	73	33	65	25
26	58	18	50	1	42	74	34	66
67	27	59	10	51	2	43	75	35
36	68	19	60	11	52	3	44	76
77	28	69	20	61	12	53	4	45

Applicable gematria tables: Pythagorean, Classical, English (for English table: from N upwards, divide by three)

Kamea of Mercury

8	58	59	5	4	62	63	1
49	15	14	52	53	11	10	56
41	23	22	44	45	19	18	48
32	34	35	29	28	38	39	25
40	26	27	37	36	30	31	33
17	47	46	20	21	43	42	24
9	55	54	12	13	51	50	16
64	2	3	61	60	6	7	57

Applicable gematria tables: Pythagorean, Classical, English (for English table: from K upwards, divide by three)

Kamea of Venus

22	47	16	41	10	35	4
5	23	48	17	42	11	29
30	6	24	49	18	36	12
13	31	7	25	43	19	37
38	14	32	1	26	44	20
21	39	8	33	2	27	45
46	15	40	9	34	3	28

Applicable gematria tables: Pythagorean, Classical

Kamea of Mars

11	24	7	20	3
4	12	25	8	16
17	5	13	21	9
10	18	1	14	22
23	6	19	2	15

Applicable gematria tables: Pythagorean, Classical (for the letter Z use 8)

Kamea of Jupiter

4	14	15	1
9	7	6	12
5	11	10	8
16	2	3	13

Applicable gematria tables: Pythagorean

Kamea of Saturn

4	9	2
3	5	7
8	1	6

Applicable gematria table: Pythagorean.

In order to create a kamea sigil, start with stages 1 and 2. We will use the Statement of Intent "My sigils work", which gives us the formula MSGLWRK (yes, now it's deliberately without the Y).

Stage 3
Choose a planet whose properties align with your intent (see page 74). We will use Saturn, for its ability to remove or get around obstacles will strengthen our Statement of Intent.

Stage 4
Pick any of the applicable gematria tables from the previous paragraph, and convert the letters of your formula into digits. The only gematria table that is applicable to the kamea of Saturn is the Pythagorean, so we will use that. Our number sequence is 4 1 7 3 5 9 2. Please note that you do not have to chaosize the digits.

Stage 5
Take a sheet of white paper and place it over the kamea of Saturn in this book, so you can see the kamea through the paper. Now, draw a circle on the first digit of your sequence. In our case, it's the number 4:

④	9	2
3	5	7
8	1	6

Stage 6

Draw a line from the circle to the next digit, and from there to the next, and from there to the next, until you reach the final digits, where you end with a line:

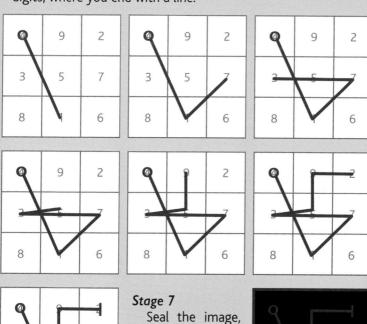

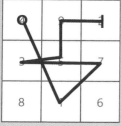

Stage 7

Seal the image, fortify the sigil (we have use a photograph of Saturn for that purpose), and then charge it.

In the case of consecutive duplicate digits, you can either decide to delete the duplicates (recommended when the kamea is small and/or there are many digits), or you can use a hump to represent the digits. So 4 1 7 7 3 5 9 makes:

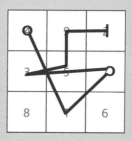

In the case of a having to pass the same point (as in our example, where we went from 7, over 5, to 3, and then back to 5), for aesthetics it's usually nicer to make a second line like in the example, but you can also trace the first line if you prefer.

Correspondences

In the table of correspondences on page 74 you can find the correspondences to the different planets. For example, if you're creating a sigil using the square of Jupiter you may decide to make the sigil in the colour purple, as this is Jupiter's colour. You may decide to make it or charge it at a particular time of day, to coincide with the hours of day associated with Jupiter, perhaps even using tin to make an amulet. In our example, we have added a photograph of Saturn underneath.

Sometimes two celestial bodies apply, for instance with the Statement of Intent "Love rules the world". It then depends on what you want to emphasize: pick Venus to emphasize love, or the Sun to emphasize ruling.

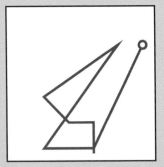 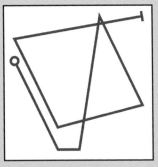

Left: "Love rules the world" on Kamea of the Sun. *Right*: "Love rules the world" on Kamea of Venus. The images were generated using https://www.chaostarot.com/app.

Personal use

You can also use kameas to sigilise your name, to infuse yourself with the quality of the planet. In this case, do not delete the vowels. If, for example, you want to be more courageous and assertive, choose the kamea of Mars.

For our example we are using the name Matthew, and we code it with the classical cypher table: 13 1 20 20 8 5 23. We will use Mars' colour red, see image.

If you want to do this with the names of other people, we recommend only using the kamea of Venus, for you are sigilising your relationship with the other person, and using the kamea of Mars, for instance, could mean your relationship becomes more competitive or even combative.

You can download a complimentary PDF with the kameas from www.palaysia.com/sigilextras.

Double sigil

If you are creating a large size sigil, consider making a double sigil. You do this by taking either the basic or the gematria sigil, and then superimpose the kamea sigil on it. You may want to simplify your basic or gematria sigil first. The beauty of this comes out through using different colours for the basic or gematria sigil, and the kamea sigil. Also, you

can now use two correspondences: in our example of "My sigils work" we have used Ceres (harvest and result) for the letter sigil, and Saturn (mastery and overcoming obstacles) for the kamea sigil, see image.

Verbal sigils

You can think of a verbal sigil as a magic spell, mantra or hidden affirmation. In fact, all magic spells are verbal sigils. You invoke your desire into being by proclaiming it out loud, and chanting or repeating the verbal sigil aloud or in your head.

After you have done the Protocol of Intent to create your Statement of Intent, you use all its letters (so including the consonants) to create a fictitious anagram that works for you. In other words, chaosize the letters. You do not need to create actual words – your sigil will be more effective when you make up the words. Take your time and enjoy the creative process!

For example:

Statement of Intent:	Peace in the world
Verbal sigil:	Plor weti dace hen
or	Hicer lot dawpene

The charging of a verbal sigil is different to the methods we've discussed. A verbal sigil needs to be repeated multiple times, and preferably over the course of multiple days, for it to be charged. You can chant, sing, think or speak the sigil. The process of repeating the sigil will get you into an altered state of mind, and that will transfer energy into the sigil. You can do this in your meditation practice, or during a walk in nature, for example. After you feel that the sigil has been charged sufficiently, you can either stop or continue to repeat it, as you please, as in the Meme and Expose methods of charging.

Alternatively, you can set up a ritual in which you proclaim the sigil a single, final time out loud. In this ritual, you may want to use a wand if you have one, to direct your spoken sigil into the universe. After that, never repeat the sigil again.

Another way to charge a verbal sigil is to proclaim it to someone else, and use them as your witness, or proclaim it to someone else when they are the beneficiary of your sigil (for example, to safeguard your children).

Computer generated sigils

Apart from creating your sigil on your computer using graphic software, you can also get your sigil generated, either online in your browser or through an app for your smart phone or tablet. Online generators include:

- https://www.chaostarot.com/app
- http://www.sigilscribe.me
- https://www.sigilengine.com

Smart phone apps include Sigil Music, Sigil Maker Free, Sigil, Chaos Magick, Sigil Automaton and Sigil Suite. Check your app store or play store.

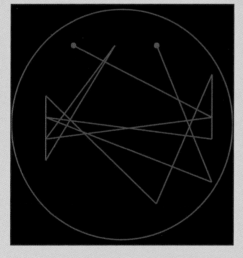

The image was generated using the Sigil Suite app with the Statement of Intent "computer generated sigils work".

If you have done the Protocol of Intent and repeated it at least twice, there should be no reason why computer generated sigils shouldn't work. And when you don't have any paper on you, or are otherwise incapable of drawing a sigil, they can be a great way to create sigils. We do, however, recommend not to use it out of fear of your own lack of creativity – effective sigils do not need to be beautiful, they need your creative energy. The same goes for when you want to hurry through the process and get it over with – effective sigils need your input, time and energy. So when you do use a computer generated sigil, be present, take your time, and feel your desire as you input your Statement of Intent.

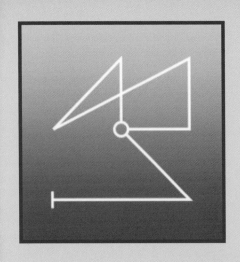

This image was generated using Sigilscribe.me with the Statement of Intent "awake and full of energy".

Video sigils

Taking it a step further, you can use your computer to create sigil videos using audio and several layers of (moving) images that are superimposed on one another.

Jesse Lee Alexander does a great job in this video where he combines the video of a burning candle, the image of the planet Mars and the First Pentacle of Mars sigil (for gaining courage, ambition, enthusiasm and all physical accomplishments), and uses the cosmic octave frequency of Mars for audio. Watch the video – with headphones – here:

https://youtu.be/YX3PhVQPhb4

Watch his video with the sigil for astral vision and the Fifth Pentacle of Jupiter – with headphones – here:

https://youtu.be/Y1iETNCI-SE

More!

If you enjoy making sigils, and the art and creativity that goes into it, you'll like to here about more methods for making sigils. Go to www.palaysia.com/sigilextras to get a PDF to learn how to make Cistercian sigils and the find your sigils' Magic Number. I have also written an e-book on progressive sigils that you can order from that site.

A word of caution

I must say at this point more does not equal better. Adding more and more stuff on top of what you're doing does not necessarily mean that your sigil will be more effective. The most important part of the entire process is the Protocol of Intent. These questions are non-negotiable and must be run again and again and again to define your true intent. The sigil is merely the icing on the cake, the detail, and as such you don't need to worry too much about whether you're getting it right, and you certainly do not need to create multiple sigils for the same Statement of Intent – unless in the process of finding the right image, but then charge only that one.

It's great to experiment with several alternatives, but do so with different Statements of Intent. Once you've gotten acquainted with several ways to create and charge sigils, you will most probably default to the one or two methods that suit you best. At this point it is interesting to note that people are generally more relaxed about the creation process when the outcome is not that important, but when they attach importance to the fulfilment of the desire and the lust of result becomes strong, they tend to feel the need to pick exactly the right methods for creating and charging the sigil. If your intuition doesn't lead you to the right method without you having to think about it or without making a conscious decision, then work on bringing down your lust of result and/or default to your favourite method of creation and charging.

If the idea of making extremely complex sigil structures appeals to you, then do so. If, like me, you're a minimalist and you prefer to be extremely simple and straightforward, then a sigil drawn by pencil on a scrap of paper is equally useful. People get caught up in technical details that don't matter. This is known in weightlifting as majoring in the minors: concentrating on the small details that are not as important as the heavy lifting. The heavy lifting is the Protocol of Intent, the repeated extrapolation of answers: what does this mean to me, how am I going to do it, what's stopping me? These things will get to the heart of your current beliefs and help you alter them. Sigils are simply tools to nudge probability in your favour.

If you are spending a lot of time dithering around about, for example, which colour you should be using on your sigil, you probably need to run the questions again.

Kamea sigil to attract love, sealed with angelic sigils, by Christian Jiminez.

Sigil for protection, by Marckus Antuan.

6. WHERE TO USE YOUR SIGILS

If you have not used the Fire & Forget category of charging methods, you can actually employ your sigils for your, or the world's benefit. In the part on charging in a previous chapter, we have discussed ways of charging your sigil by exposing it to other people. In this chapter, it's not about charging your (private) sigil, but about influencing others with your sigils – because indeed, it is very possible to influence others with your sigils.

Now as you may understand, this is an ethical question. Even though I'm about to give you some guidelines, ultimately it is up to you to find where your personal boundaries are in employing sigils for this reason. The sigil next to this paragraph is a benevolent sigil, and I am employing it to program your unconscious to only use sigils for the good of all. **You can freely spread a sigil:**

• *when it is idealistic, benevolent and benefits our planet and all of its inhabitants*
  For example:
  • Peace on earth
  • A safe home for all children
  • Freedom for women worldwide
  • Let love guide you
  • Focus on the good in others
  • Protection

• *when, in specific instances, you want others to perform a certain kind of behaviour, that is beneficial to them*
  For example:
  • Concentrate (for example on a book cover)

- Heal, live, and love life (for example in a hospital)
- Peace and respect (for example in a football stadium)
- Calm and clear-headed (for example during an exam)

- *when it could benefit others, while benefiting you*
    For example:
    - My hands help you heal
    - This product helps you achieve ...
    - Use this book to learn about ...

- *with the knowledge and approval of person in question*

Use your own judgement and ethics to spread a sigil:

- *when the scale shifts more towards your own benefit*
    For example:
    - Subscribe to my You Tube channel
    - Buy this product
    - The winner of this game is [enter your name] (for example to influence your opponent in sports)

> *In stead (or also), make a sigil that focusses on you, and then expose it to others purely for the purpose of charging. Using the examples above: I have ten thousand subscribers to my You Tube channel; The sales of my product earn me a good living; I win at ...*

- *when you intend to help specific others, without their knowledge and approval, and without you knowing for certain this is what they want themselves*
    For example:
    - Release your need for validation
    - Lose weight
    - Peace and quiet (for example for noisy neighbours)
    - Safety and protection

> *In stead (or also), make a sigil that focusses on you letting go of the need for others to change, and then expose it to others purely for the purpose of charging. For example: My wife finds validation in herself (or better still: I allow my wife her needs); My brother's weight is perfect for him; I find peace and quiet whatever happens.*

• **when you can't claim absolute truth or can't give guarantees:**
> For example:
> • My hands heal you (as opposed to "my hands help you heal")
> • This product is the best for you

> *In stead (or also), make a sigil that focusses on your underlying desires, and then expose it to others purely for the purpose of charging. For example: My target customers find me easily; My product is effective; Customers love my product and keep buying.*

Do not use sigils:

• **when you want others to do something that takes away their freedom of choice**
> For example:
> • Love me (to make a person fall in love with you)

> *In stead, make a sigil that focusses on you, and then expose it to others purely for the purpose of charging. For example: I am worthy of love; I have a lasting, loving relationship.*

• **when you have negative or malevolent intentions**

In stead, make sigils to heal yourself and to be successful yourself. Remember, the best revenge is not spending energy on others, only on your healing and growth for an inevitable successful, fulfilling and rewarding life.

Placing your sigil

Now that you have decided to spread your sigil, use any of these options, or think up other ways to expose it to the world. Obviously, you can use any sigil and place it anywhere, but I have added specific ideas for use in specific placements.

- Front door or facade of your house
  Use sigils for protection, safety, love and harmony to influence people who approach or enter your house. Alternatively, place the sigil for your family purpose, mission or core values here (see chapter eight).
- Rooms in your house
  Use sigils that help the function of the room, for example:
    ○ *love and relaxation* or *tidy and clean* for the living room
    ○ *harmony, warmth and good conversations* for the dining room
    ○ *intimacy and deep rest* in the bedroom
    ○ *change toilet paper when empty* in the toilet
- Bumper sticker
  Use sigils that encourage safety, calmness and focus.
- Engrave or inscribe
  Place the sigil on ritual tools like wands, or tools that others use often, like pens.
- Digital placement
  In the section on charging we've already discussed digital placements of your sigil, they apply here as well.
- Advertisement

You can add the sigil to any advertising you do, online or offline.

- Mail

  Add the sigil to postcards and letters you send out, either in the letter itself or on the envelop. Or, print postcards with your sigil on it and send out to family and friends.

- Clothing & bags

  Have your sigil printed on your own clothing, caps or bags, or sell these items with your sigil on it.

- Gifts

  You can have personalized gifts made with your sigil printed on it, like baby rompers, mugs, notebooks, key chains, etcetera. These make beautiful presents for newborns, children of all ages and adults.

- Store or office

  Place the sigil on the door of your store or office.

- Product placement

  If you sell physical products, you can have your sigil printed on the packaging, or on the product itself.

- Logo

  If you have a business, in a way your logo is already a type of sigil, but you can use a specific sigil as your logo was well. You can either sigilise the name of your business or the mission of your business, to use as your logo.

- Natural elements

  Carve your sigil on natural elements like a tree or rock in your garden, facing the street or sidewalk so passers-by can see it. Do not carve your sigil into a tree or rock when it is not on your own property (and if it is, without consent of the tree or rock).

- Sign

  Place the sigil on a sign in your garden, in your shop window, on the outside wall of your house or office, etcetera.

When you place a sigil on something, especially when doing it digitally, you have the option of making the sigil almost invisible, by decreasing the opacity of the sigil. Or, you can use invisible ink to make your sigil. This way, the sigil will not interfere with the design of whatever is underneath. This is also a good way of masking them if you don't want the public to know that you are using sigils.

7. SOME CONSIDERATIONS

You can make as many sigils as you want at a time – in fact, is preferable to make more than one as long as they have different Statements of Intent. The thing to look out for is that your sigils don't contradict one another. This may sound obvious, but needs careful consideration.

When will my sigil work?

One of the most often asked questions is how much time it takes for a sigil to work. There is no clear answer to that question – a sigil can work as fast as a few hours, sometimes it takes a few months – regardless of the type or difficulty or your Statement of Intent.

My general rule is that if a sigil hasn't worked within three months, you should revisit the Protocol of Intent. Your initial desire may have remained the same, but your Statement of Intent needs careful reconsideration. Do not redo the sigil with the same Statement of Intent – really dive into the Protocol and create a new, perhaps more accurate, Statement of Intent.

'The bushes in our front garden had been eaten by insects, and I did a sigil for it to restore and get its leaves back. But by next spring, nothing had happened and I ended up working with a new Statement of Intent, something like beautiful bushes in our front garden without me having to do any heavy work. About a week later one of my neighbours said he was going to rent a mechanical digger for his garden, and wanted to know if I wanted my hedge removed. He did all the heavy work for me, all I had to do was buy and plant new bushes.' –Dennis

Creating a unique sigil

If you've made a sigil for a specific Statement of Intent, we cannot stress how important it is not to make a second sigil, no matter how much time has past since. This notion usually gets people apprehensive, worried that they have to get it right the first time. Let us start by stating: you cannot do it wrong. But other than that, it is a good thing since it forces you to narrow down what it is you want.

For some sigils, you are likely to have them for the remainder of your life, take for example "Ease and confidence in public speaking". But if you have a specific event coming up, you may want to create a sigil that is specifically targeted at and narrowed down to that event. That way, you don't have to worry about having used your one chance at a sigil on that topic. Say, for example, you need money to buy a car. You could do a sigil on money, but it would be much smarter to do a sigil on the car directly.

Having said that, you might forget ever having made a sigil on a specific Statement of Intent. If it manifested, there is no need for a new sigil anyway, but if it never manifested and you truly can't remember doing a sigil on it, there is no harm in doing a further one – to your conscious brain it will be the first.

'I hardly ever do money and prosperity sigils. Partly, because I when I am going to create one, I want to get it just right. But mainly it is because I think it makes more sense to do specific sigils on what I would use the money for. So, for example, I have created sigils for easily affording the monthly house payments, a new car, a family holiday, a crystal, provide aid to a charity, a new phone, and so on.' –Aedith Empress

Undoing sigils

At one point, you may need to undo a specific sigil – desires can change both before and after they are fulfilled. Luckily, there is no need for any specific ritual, and even if you've forgotten that the sigil on display in your living room is actually the one you want to undo, there is no problem. The only thing you need to do to undo a sigil is create a new one with a Statement of Intent that specifies your current wish. In other words, do not create a sigil for undoing a sigil. Just identify your new desire, and do the Protocol of Intent.

Say, for example, you want to undo the sigil that had the Statement of Intent "I live in an apartment in the city centre", because now you have a family, you want to move into a house with a garden in a quieter neighbourhood. Your new Statement of Intent could be "We live in a spacious house in a kids-friendly area". Simply create a sigil for that, charge it, and forget about it. Your earlier sigil will be undone and overwritten by the new one.

Custom made sigils

Not everyone can, or wants to create a sigil themselves. Sometimes it's useful to get someone else to craft a sigil for you, especially if you feel that you have lust of result around the issue or that you cannot get the kind of aesthetic that you're after.

After you have received the sigil, you will still need to charge it yourself, but first you need to connect your energy to it. Depending on whether or not the sigil has been sealed by the one who made it, start by adding a seal (see page 71). Gaze or stare at the sigil without focussing on it, while holding in your mind a vision of your life with the desire fulfilled, and building inside you the feeling of fulfilment, ease, joy, relaxation and pride you would feel upon your desire being met. Do this for a minimum of 66 seconds (you may set an alarm). Then, trace the lines with your eyes, while thinking "It is done" and expanding the feeling of fulfilment to outside your body. After that, use any of the methods for charging mentioned in stage 8.

On my website www.thechaoschamber.com there is the chance for you to help me design a sigil with you or for you.

 This comes with a consultation to make sure that your Statement of Intent lines up with what you really want. I also offer a print on demand service for the crafting of amulets and items of clothing with your personal sigil. Visit the website to find out more.

Tracking

As stated before, it is necessary that you forget about (the Statement of Intent of) a sigil after you have destroyed or displayed it. You can, however, track the results of your sigil. Doing this, and seeing your sigils really do work, will give you more confidence in creating your next sigil *and* increase the power of your sigils. In a notebook you keep specifically for this purpose, write down the Statement of Intent and the date on a new page – do not draw the sigil itself there. When you add a new entry, go to a new page immediately so you don't look at the previous entries. Take out your notebook once every three to six months, read your previous Statement of Intents and write down any comments. Or, when you know a certain Statement of Intent has materialised, find it in your notebook and write down the (approximate) date it materialised.

8. OTHER SIGILS

Hopefully we have clearly explained that you make sigils for the manifestation of your desires. These desires can range from physical, material things, to states of mind, to atmospheres in a room or at an event, to health, to behaviour, to ideas, to finding help or to helping others, to emotional states, to solutions, to achievements, to overcoming challenges, to getting a lucky break, to finding something lost, to idealistic causes, to spiritual states, and so on – the list is endless.

But apart from desires, you can make sigils for other things like:
- Your soul's purpose
- Your soul's mission
- Your life vision
- Your core values
- Your first name, last name or full name
- Your guardian angel or spirit guide (you can use the sigil to invoke their energy in your meditation or when performing a ritual)
- Your family's purpose, mission statement, vision and core values
- Your family's last names (combine father's last name and mother's last name)
- Your relationship's purpose, mission statement, vision and core values
- Your business's purpose, mission statement, vision, core values and name (if you have your own business or are self-employed)
- Your company's purpose, mission statement, vision and core values (if you are employed)
- The purpose, mission statement, vision and core values of a charity, foundation, group or sports club you are involved with
- The purpose, mission statement, vision and core values – or what you feel they should be – of the city, state, or country where you live, or of our planet

A purpose is the reason(s) why you exist. A mission is what you bring to the world, or how you serve the world (or a specific group). A vision is your highest aspiration in life, what you ideally want to be (and thus could also be called a desire). Core values are your guiding principles. A person or business typically has around seven core values, for example integrity, harmony, independence, excellence.

Download the complimentary exercise to discover your core values from www.palaysia.com/sigilextras ·

The purpose of the company that publishes this book is to spread wisdom and increase vibration worldwide. Their mission is to inspire and empower people to live their soul's mission with books, courses and other products or services that liberate, raise vibration and provide positive life tools. Their vision is to be a powerful and effective driving force in the world for soul-led living and vibrational elevation. Their core values are transformation, love, excellence, joy, aesthetics, progressiveness and integrity.

You can create a family crest from the sigil your make for your family's name or other attributes.

Since the attributes mentioned here are not a desire, you don't need to run the Protocol of Intent on them, but we do recommend that you examine and question the purpose, mission, vision and core values to arrive at the right statements for your sigils.

9. SIGILS OF CONNECTION

Over the centuries, many sigils have been created to represent entities, deities, spirits or thought forms. There are sigils for archangel Michael, for the planet Arcturus, for rain, etcetera.

Sigils like these function like telephone numbers for establishing energetic connections, and they are part of ceremonial magic (in stead of chaos magic).

A selection of these sigils has been included in this book for your benefit. Please note that these sigils do not need to be charged or activated to work.

You can use these sigils in three ways:
- To evoke the energy or presence of an entity into a ritual
- To establish a connection to energetically communicate with, or channel an entity
- To connect to an entity on a more ongoing basis, for example by placing the sigil on a visible place in your house or wear it as jewellery

To work with any of the sigils in this chapter in a ritual or for communication, you can work with an existing copy of the sigil, or but it's recommended to redraw the sigil yourself to connect to the entity or the intent. Add a seal if it hasn't got one yet. Then, gaze or stare at the sigil without focussing on it, while holding in your mind a vision of the entity or energy you want to establish connection with.

Solomon's Sigil

A specific sigil for powerful manifestation and protection is the sigil now known as the "Seal of Solomon".

According to the Jewish bible, the Old Testament, the Quran and the Hadiths, Solomon was a wise King and son of King David. His reigns is thought to be from 970 to 931 B.C. and he is known for his occult or magic powers. It is believed that while

Solomon's Sigil in an amulet, made from an old Brazilean coin. Created by Marcel Ácrata, who makes custom made sigil amulets via www.facebook.com/marcelo.c.dalto

in trance, Solomon received a sigil. He had it engraved into a ring (the Talmud reads of a ring with the divine name) and with this magic ring he could command good and evil spirits, thus giving him tremendous manifestation powers. This ring was known as the Seal of Solomon, seal meaning signet ring, and this name is now also used for the sigil. The hexagram or "Star of David", which in our times is a symbol for Judaism and sits on the Israeli flag, has its origins in 14th-century depictions of the Seal of Solomon, but the main difference between the two is that the Seal of Solomon is three-dimensional, the two triangles being intertwined.

The Key of Solomon

The "Key of Solomon" is a grimoire or magic book, that is attributed to King Solomon, but scholars agree was written in the 14th century, during the Renaissance, in Italy. It is, however, based on (many) earlier Jewish kabbalist and Arab magic texts, which in turn are likely to be derived from ancient knowledge. Many different versions of the book are in existence.

In the book are instructions to make sigils (named pentacles in the book) for different intentions like how to be invisible, how to recover stolen or lost items, how to make someone fall in love with you, against adversity, for wealth and prosperity, etcetera. As you can see, quotations from the Bible are used in the seals of the sigils. It is possible that these were only added to gain the approval of the church and to avoid persecution.

There is a further grimoire called "The Lesser Keys of Solomon" which focusses more on demonology.

Original sigil or pentacle from the grimoire "The key of Solomon": the fifth pentacle of the Sun, "It serveth to invoke those spirits who can transport thee from one place unto another, over a long distance and in short time." The seal reads: "Angelis suis mandabit de te ut custodiant te in omnibus viis tuis in manibus portabunt te" which means "He shall give his angels charge over thee, to keep thee in all thy ways. They shall bear thee up in their hands". You can find the entire grimoire and all its pentacles via: http://www.esotericarchives.com/solomon/ksol.htm

Modern rendition of a sigil or pentacle from the grimoire "The key of Solomon": the first pentacle of Venus, "It serveth to to control the Spirits of Venus, and especially those herein written." See the table of correspondences for Venus on page 74 for the use of this sigil.

Sigillum Dei

The Sigillum Dei or "Sigil of Source" contains the names of Source and angels. The function of this sigil is to have power over all forces except Archangels, but this power is only attainable for those with pure, Source-inspired intentions, also called beatific visionaries. Nowadays, the sigil is used to induce visions, elicit benevolent entities for the purpose of channelling and to evoke benevolent spirits. The sigil can also be use to charge crystals. The sigil is also know under the name of Sigillum Æmeth, or Sigil of Truth.

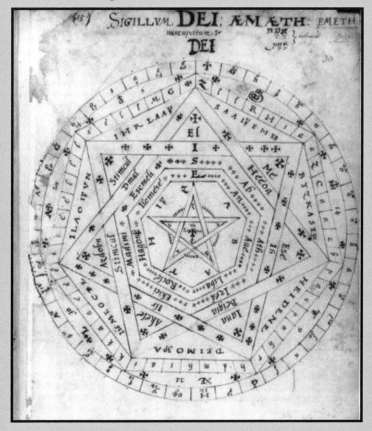

Selection of sigils

Sigil for protection

Sigil to stop procrastinating
on Almandine crystal

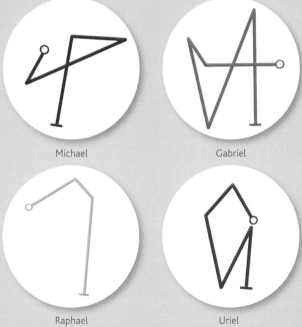

Sigil for clarity

Archangel Sigils

Michael

Gabriel

Raphael

Uriel

Interstellar Sigils

ARCTURUS

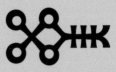

SIRIUS

ALDEBARAN

VEGA

ORION

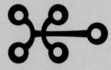

SPICA

ANTARES

DENEB ALGEDI

ALPHECCA

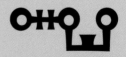

THE PLEÏADES

Sigil for prosperity

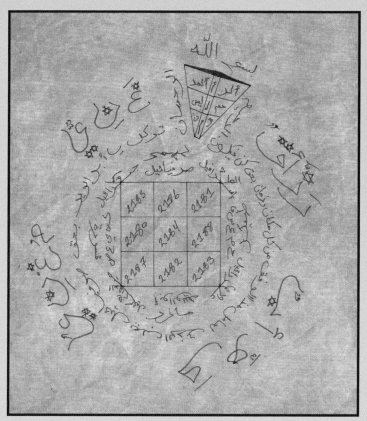

Arabic sigil for prosperity, created for this book by Reda Ben Adam. This seal uses 4 names of Source: Wahhab the bestower, Razzaq the sustainer, Ghaniy the rich, Moughniyy the enricher. Within the square a prayer is made for its wearer using those divine names, so it is to be worn upon oneself.

ABOUT THE AUTHOR

Mark Vincent is a professional musician of 25 years, a clinical hypnotherapist with over 15 years experience, and an experienced chaos magician. He draws upon his extensive knowledge of neuroscience, psychology and therapeutic approaches to develop cutting-edge occult methods to ensure more effective spell-casting. He runs numerous (online) workshops through Treadwell's, including:

• The Chaos Chambers (a four-part system of chaos magic)
• Hypnosis and Trance for Magical Practice
• Practical Magic: Creating a Servitor
• Sigil Crafting
• Uncovering Your True Intention
• Hypnosis for Occult Practice

Mark specialises in finding out what people really want versus what they think they want and then teaching them to employ various occult approaches to enact their will. As well as chaos magic, Mark is an experienced Enochian magic and various non-traditional occult approaches. His methods can be integrated and used by people who are working in established traditions as well as by solo practitioners.

Mark also offers one-to-one sessions for those who wish to go deeper, and personalised sigil creation.

FOR MARK'S CLASSES AND WORKSHOPS, GO TO:

https://www.treadwells-london.com/mark

FOR PRIVATE CONSULTATIONS, PERSONALISED SIGILS, AND SIGIL APPAREL:

https://www.thechaoschamber.com

TO BUY THIS BOOK, GO TO:

http://www.thesigilsecret.com

FOR THE COMPLIMENTARY EXTRAS WITH THIS BOOK:

https://www.palaysia.com/sigilextras

'The gift of a class with Mark is he doesn't just show you how to create a Sigil, he pierces through all illusion and confusion to explain why it works.' –Gemma

'It was easy to follow, and the structure of talking about the underlying mental things in the first part was great.' –Åskar

'I rarely listen to anyone, but Mark can cut through all my bullshit excuses and reach the core of what it is I should focus on. Thanks to him, I feel more confident in myself and my work – and I also make more money! And it's not just that he helped me in the moment, he gave me the tools to be able to help myself in the future, too.' –Amanda

'Thank you for an excellent few evenings of seminars. I have come away from the two days with new knowledge and ideas, and confirmation that at least some of the things I'm doing are "right".' –Zach

Order your sigil products from **WWW.THESIGILSECRET.COM**

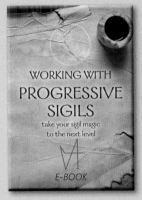

WORKING WITH
**PROGRESSIVE
SIGILS**
take your sigil magic
to the next level

E-BOOK

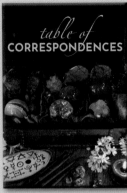

table of
CORRESPONDENCES

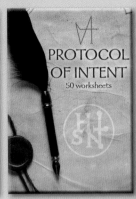

**PROTOCOL
OF INTENT**
50 worksheets

MORE FROM *palaysia*

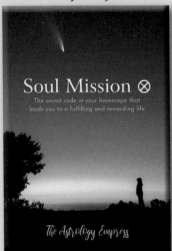

Soul Mission ⊗
The secret code in your horoscope that
leads you to a fulfilling and rewarding life

The Astrology Empress

With this book you've got the code to find,
understand and live your Soul Mission.

'It's spot on – how bizarre!'

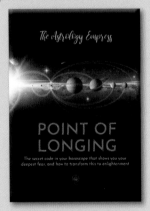

The Astrology Empress

**POINT OF
LONGING**
The secret code in your horoscope that shows you your
deepest fear, and how to transform this to enlightenment

Simple step-by-step plan,
anyone can do it!

*'Oh wow! This is so true! I am very
much looking for meaning: who am
I and why was I put on this earth?
This is book is super valuable.'*

Newly discovered
horoscope point!

*'It was quite confronting,
but very liberating! This is
exactly what continuously
causes problems in my life.'*

Watch the videos at
WWW.LIVEYOURSOULMISSION.COM